Sugar Art Creations
Floral Art

by Helen Dissell and Gill Pope

Acknowledgements

The inspiration to write a book on sugar floral art came about through the dedication and passion which our tutor, the late Gladiola Botha, instilled in us from our early days in decorating. We would like to dedicate this book to her.

Helen & Gill

To my dear late mother, Jean Sweetman, who encouraged perfection, determination and ambition in me from childhood. Thank you, Mom.

My loving husband Ralph, my best critic and advisor, I thank you for your patience and support for the past fifteen years.

Gill, we have walked the path in friendship and skills growth – learning and laughing all the way. You are a true inspiration, a special friend and an invaluable co-author and there is never a dull moment – thank you for always being there, cake sister!

Shane Pope and Bronwyn McCann – many thanks for the hours of work you have dedicated to our photography and editorial comment. It is greatly appreciated.

Finally, acknowledgments to the SACDG (South African Cake Decorators Guild) and QCDA Inc (Queensland Cake Decorators Guild of Australia), students past and present, my sister Bev, my family Zoe and Ryan and my previous employer, Dr Mervyn Sender, for the encouragement and support I have received from all of you in your individual ways.

Helen Dissell

To my cake sister Helen, whose support, understanding, laughter and joy kept me going late into the night, I would never have been able to do this without you. And to her husband Ralph for being our financial advisor, for providing support – and for feeding us when we forgot to eat.

To my dear kind and patient husband and photographer, Shane, whose eye for detail made me re-do countless pieces, until he was satisfied with the work.

To my family, my sister Dr J, who gave us unlimited psychological support and vitamins, and her husband Guy, who provided lots of advice.

To my dear Mom, who read notes and listened to hours of explanations on cakes. The best mom ever.

To the SACDG for always being there. I have made so many friends through the guild, both here and in Australia. Special thanks to Anne Horner of Chefs and Icers in South Africa.

To my friends, Jenny and Rene, and my god-daughter Karen for all the publishing advice and art direction – award winning publishers themselves – thank you so much for your guidance.

Lastly, to my brother Clive and his wife Sandy, for providing gallons of wine and listening to hours of book conversation.

Gill Pope

First published in Australia in 2010 by
SugarArtCreations Pty Ltd
PO Box 634
Sanctuary Cove Queensland 4212 Australia
ABN 60 135 287 482

Sanctuary Cove Publishing Pty Ltd
PO Box 252
Sanctuary Cove Queensland 4212 Australia
ABN 99 424 098 773

Copyright © SugarArtCreations Pty Ltd 2010
Design Copyright © Sanctuary Cove Publishing Pty Ltd 2010

Authors:	Helen Dissell and Gill Pope
Photography:	Shane Pope
	Mark Burgin
Art Direction:	April Williams
Copy Editor:	Rhonda Oxnam
Graphic Design:	Jenna Moir
	and Alisha Stanley
Consulting Editor:	Clare E. Urwin
Editorial Assistant:	Yvonne Gramstad

Produced in China by APOL.

The rights of SugarArtCreations Pty Ltd and the photographers of this work have been asserted by them under the *Copyright Amendment (Moral Rights) Act (2000)*.

This work is copyright. All rights reserved apart from any use as permitted under the *Copyright Act 1968*, no part may be reproduced, copied, scanned, stored in a retrieval system, recorded or transmitted in any form or by any means, without the prior written permission of the publisher.

Sugar Art Creations – Floral Art
ISBN 978-0-646-53320-9 (Hardback)
1. Crafts (Sugar Art) 2. Food and Drink (Sugar Art) 3. Hobbies (Sugar Art)

On the cover: Quirky Cake, page 100.

Sugar Art Creations

Floral Art

by Helen Dissell and Gill Pope

Sugar Art creations

www.sugarartcreations.com.au

Foreword

Helen Dissell

Gill Pope

Helen Dissell and Gill Pope are two good friends who share a passion for the wonderful craft of sugar art. They first met in cake decorating class 15 years ago and, since then, they have travelled the world learning new skills and keeping abreast of international techniques and standards.

Inspired by the late Gladiola Botha and taught by 'Ma Botha' and the South African Cake Decorating Guild (SACDG), Helen and Gill are both qualified teachers and judges in sugar art and train students in sugar and chocolate work in Australia and South Africa.

What started out as a hobby has now became a profession, with the 'cake sisters' starting their company, SugarArtCreations, ten years ago despite being separated by thousands of miles – Helen lives in Australia, while Gill resides in South Africa.

Gill and Helen are members of the SACDG, the Australian Cake Decorators Association and the British Sugar Guild, and are passionate about marrying new and old techniques while continuing to strive for perfection in both the visual appeal and culinary delight of this wonderful art form.

The decision to commit their designs to paper was born over numerous cups of coffee and glasses of Champagne. Notes and ideas were put into place, then, through modern technology (including thousands of Skype calls and emails), ideas and concepts evolved.

Helen and Gill have taken a more modern, contemporary approach in design by incorporating 'fashionable' decorating techniques with their own unique form of expression. They hope their book, Sugar Art Creations – Floral Art, will inspire many new and enthusiastic cake decorators as well as offering their colleagues a fresh insight into what can be achieved with talent, patience and attention to detail.

Although presented as a 'collection', the 12 cakes were carefully chosen to illustrate a variety of styles and techniques, as well as showcasing an eclectic range of colours, designs and floral arrangements. A selection of recipes, which have been passed on from teacher to decorator, have been used, however, in some cases these recipes have been adjusted to suit the authors' personal style and creativity.

As the individual designs evolved the cakes not only took on aspects of Helen and Gill's personalities they also developed their own unique traits which are reflected in the cake names. (Readers can make up their own minds about who is the quirky one and who is more romantic!)

Both Helen and Gill are extremely honoured to present their creations and hope to inspire and delight fellow cake decorators the world over.

Contents

Equipment and Terminology	8
Cakes:	
Artistic	12
Cheerful	24
Dramatic	30
Elegant	46
Exotic	58
Flirty	76
Inspired	84
Quirky	100
Romantic	110
Serene	132
Stunning	144
Vibrant	156
Royal Icing	170
Recipe Collection	173
Troubleshooting & Helpful Hints	180
Colour & Classification	182

Artistic
Snail Creeper, Clivia, Decorative Work

Inspired
Butterfly Iris, Didgery Sticks, Dietes Flower, Jacaranda, Gum Nuts

Cheerful
Marguerite Daisy

Quirky
Spider Orchid, Stamen Extension, Tilansia (Tree Moss)

Dramatic
Alstromeria, Wildfire Hybrid Tea Rose, Monstera Deliciosa, Arum Lily, Forget-me-not, New Zealand Flax

Romantic
Open Champagne Rose, Spider Lily, Ixora, Royal Purple Liriope, Basket Weave, String of Pearls

Elegant
Flowering Plum, Indian Hawthorn, Lace Flowers

Serene
Periwinkle, Bauhinia, Oriental Stringwork

Exotic
Hibiscus, Bouganvillea, Anthirium, Frangipani, Extension and Bridge Work

Stunning
Sprekelia, Bird Flower, Sugarpaste Bows

Flirty
Fuchsia, Filigree Butterfly

Vibrant
Poinciana, Sword Fern, Russelia 'Lemon Falls', St. Joseph Lily, Lace Points

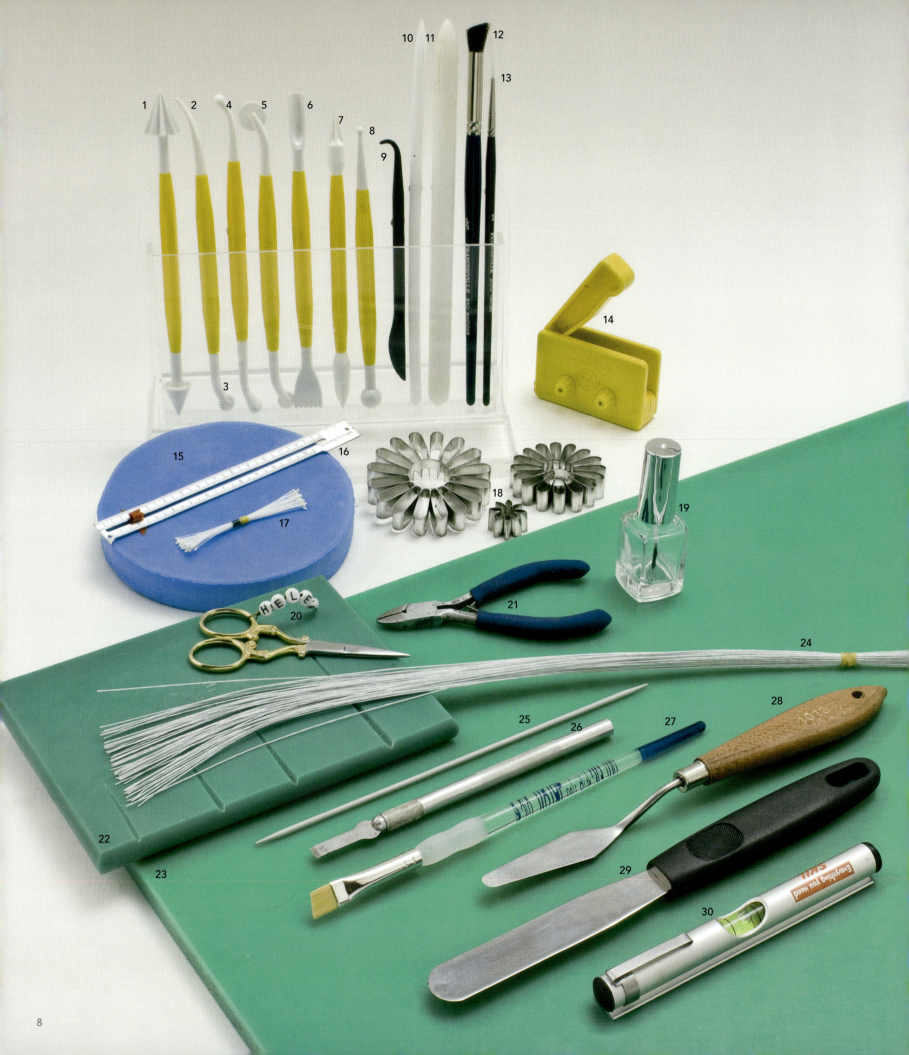

Equipment & Terminology

The modelling tools described in this section have been used throughout the book and are an indicatation of what is required in a basic modelling kit.

1. Cone tool – large/plain
2. Dresden/Veining tool
3. Stitching wheel
4. Dog bone tool
5. Cutting wheel
6. Marking tool
7. Cone tool – 5 & 6 petal
8. Balling tool
9. Jem hook tool
10. Cell stick – small
11. Cell stick – large
12. Dusting/paintbrush – flat ended
13. Dusting/paintbrush – fine pointed
14. Tape shredder
15. Balling mat
16. Ruler gauge
17. Stamens
18. Cutters
19. Tylose glue
20. Embroidery scissors
21. Wire cutters
22. Rolling board – grooved
23. Rolling board – large, non-stick
24. Covered wire
25. Sock needle
26. Scalpel
27. Dusting brush – flat ended
28. Trowel
29. Spatula
30. Spirit level

Suppliers:
Barco Powder Colours
'SugarArtCreations' cutters by Bessie
PME & Jem Tools
Bekenal piping tubes
Bakel's sugarpaste

Actiwhite
Egg white albumen which is a volumiser used in making royal icing.

Agar Agar
The vegetarian equivalent to gelatine. Can be found in Asian grocery stores.

Almond Icing
Sugarpaste which has colouring and almond essence added to it. It contains no ground nuts. Used by some decorators instead of marzipan, although this is not a good idea as it thickens the icing layer and can have a nasty flavour.

Angled tweezers
Tweezers which have a bend in the bottom of them. They are used in inserting flowers into sprays and also in pinching lines into paste.

Balling mat
Compressed foam used to thin edges of petals and give movement. It is preferable to using the palm of the hand which often sticks and tears the paste.

Balling tool/Dog bone tool
Used to thin edges and give movement to leaves and petals.

Bubble sponge
Foam sponge which has ripples in it. It can be used as mattress underlay and also in packaging.

Cell stick
A very versatile tool which is made out of compressed nylon and can be used for rolling out paste. The rounded end can be used to make the centres of orchids and as a balling tool to thin edges and create movement. The rounded edge can also be used to frill or flute edges of petals and paste.

Cellogen
This is Tylopur and is a binder in sugar mediums. When added to liquids it forms a viscous solution. It is a protective colloid or stabiliser of liquid medium giving stretch.

CMC
Carboxymethyl cellulose.

Cocoa Butter
The fat extracted from the cocoa bean used in making chocolate.

Cone tools
These tools can come in a plain cone tool or 5 or 6 petal cone tool. The cone tool is mainly used in making the centres of flowers – particularly blossoms and smaller flowers. It can also be used to mark facial features or positions where even spacing is required. Can be adapted as a frilling tool.

Confectioners glaze
Edible food grade varnish. This can be used as a preserving agent or to make items shiny. Chefs often use it to give potato chips a crisp finish and shiny gloss.

Copha
Vegetable fat.

Cornflour/corn starch
This is light fine white powder used as a thickener and stabiliser. It is also referred to as Maize flour.

Corn syrup
A runny substitute for glucose syrup.

Covered wire
Wires covered with paper. There are different thicknesses called gauges. The higher the gauge the thinner the wire. The smaller the gauge the thicker the wire.

Cutting wheel
This tool is like a pizza cutter and cuts paste easily.

Dresden/veining tool
Used to mark central veins down leaves and petals and also to mark lines or make grooves in paste or give a feathered edge to paste.

Dusting/paintbrush
Flat-ended soft bristled paintbrush.

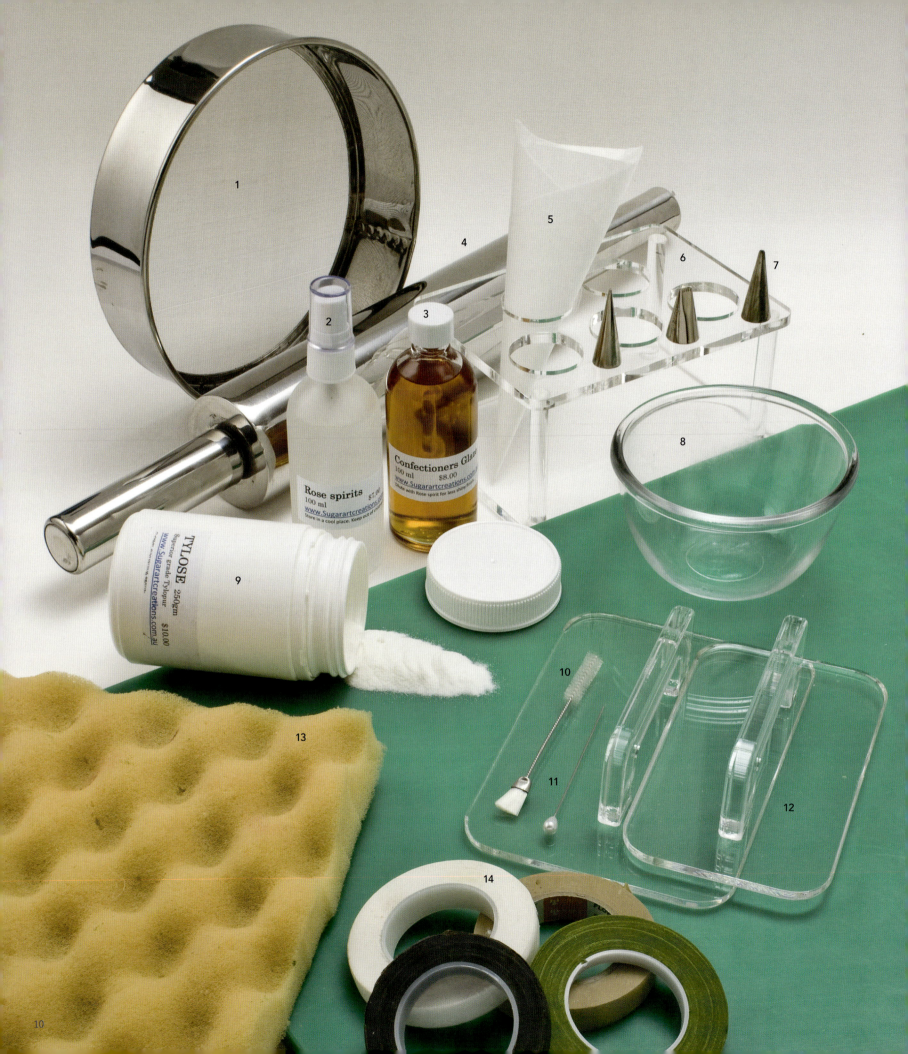

Equipment & Terminology

1. Fine sieve
2. Isopropyl alcohol (rose spirit)
3. Confectioners glaze
4. Rolling pin – large
5. Piping bag
6. Tube stand
7. Bekenal piping tubes
8. Glass mixing bowl – small
9. Tylose powder
10. Tube cleaner
11. Hat pin
12. Cake smoothers
13. Bubble sponge
14. Florist tape

Fine embroidery scissors
Small fine-bladed and pointed scissors used in cake decorating.

Flower paste
The paste used to make sugar flowers. There are many recipes. This paste can be rolled extremely thinly and has a lot of stretch.

Florist tape
The tape used to tape floral sprays and wires together. It comes in different types:
- Stemtex – a wax-like papery texture. This is good as it does not stretch or show the wires through the paper and it can be dusted the required colour.
- Parafilm – This is a plastic tape and is used mainly by florists and occasionally by some decorators.

Gum Arabic
Edible gum glue.

Gum Tragacanth
Similar to Tylose powder and also a plant extract.

Holsum
Vegetable fat – solidified white vegetable oil.

Hook Tool
This tool has a hook at one end and is used to form curves on the inner edges of petals. Also used to mark indents such as mouths.

Icing sugar mix
Icing sugar with cornflour or wheaten flour additive.

Isopropyl alcohol
Alcohol which has a high evaporation rate. Used in breaking down confectioners glaze concentrations and also to remove stains and paint with.

Liquid glucose
Also known as glucose syrup. It is a purified and thickened concentration of saccharides (sugars) obtained from starch. It helps to retain moisture and is used in candy making, baking and making jams, jellies and pastes.

Marzipan
A paste made using ground almonds – refer recipe section. Used underneath sugarpaste on cakes and also used in fillings and making chocolate delicacies.

Mexican paste
Used for architectural work and plaques. It dries very quickly and can be rolled very thinly but has little stretch. It is brittle and not suitable for making flowers.

Modelling paste
Paste used to make figurines or novelty characters, bows and drapes. It does not have a lot of stretch and is fairly pliable and easy to work with.

Non stick nylon board
Used to roll out paste very thinly. Its non-stick properties reduce the chances of the paste from breaking as you do not have to use a non stick agent such as copha or cornflower, therefore, the paste is not weakened and does not dry out quickly.

Pastillage
Has the same properties as Mexican paste.

Petal base
A combination of edible vegetable fats used in paste making and to give clean-cut edges to paste.

Pure Icing sugar
Icing sugar which has no additives.

Rose Spirit
Same as isopropyl alcohol.

Royal Icing mix
Instant royal icing powder to which you add water and beat well. It is made from dried egg white and icing sugar.

Spatula
A flat metal spatula used to mix royal icing. It is not flexible.

Stamens
Cotton lengths which have been stiffened in sugar and the ends dipped in royal icing. They are fully edible and used in the centres of sugar flowers.

Stitching tool
Used to make a stitching look in paste for decorative purposes.

Sugarpaste
A wide term for flower paste, gumpaste, fondant, modelling paste, Pettinice and plastic icing.

Trowel
This is used to pick up finely rolled flower or modelling paste. It is also used as a cutting edge or to mark grooves with.

Tylose glue
Also called gum glue. It is made from water and Tylose powder and is entirely edible.

Tylose powder (tylopur)
A sugar-shortening agent made from cellogen, an extract from a leguminous plant in the Mediterranean. There are synthetic grades called CMC which is carboxymethyl cellulose. There are different grades of this available on the market.

Artistic

The predominant colours used in this artistically inspired design are yellow, purple and pink.

Yellow clivia gives the cake vibrance, the mauve tones in the snail creeper create harmony and the touch of pink, along with green leaves, adds contrast.

The tendrils of the snail creeper ensure that the arrangement is not too structured and are in keeping with the modern contemporary angles of the cake.

This type of design is best suited to a firm cake such as carrot cake or fruit cake.

Snail creeper

page 14

Clivia

page 19

Decorative work

page 22

Snail Creeper

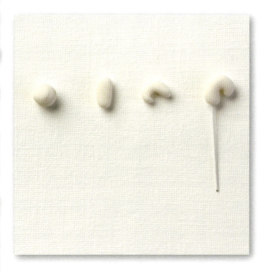

Vigna Caracalla Also commonly called Corkscrew Vine. The plant originates in tropical South America and Central America and is named after its unusual, snail-shaped flowers and buds. The creeper is fast growing and flowers from mid-summer to autumn. The blooms are about 5cm long with upper petals that contort backwards with an elongated keel, coiled in 4 or 5 corkscrew-like spirals. The fragrant flowers are a mix of magenta, mauve, blue and pink and turn yellow as they age.

Materials

White flower paste

Powder colours: Barney, turquoise, P pink, rose, yellow, lemon, lilac, viridian, lime, brown

Snow or cornflour for mixing

Tylose glue

28, 24, 22 & 20 gauge wire

Cutters or templates

Lily veiner

Balling mat

Bubble foam

Modelling tools

Buds

The buds start off small and look like little worms. They are a mix of mauve and magenta shades with light green in the middle. (See colour mixing guide.) The bigger buds curl up a bit more, in a corkscrew shape, and have green in the centre.

Small Buds

1. Use a small piece of white flower paste and roll it into a little ball.
2. Form the ball into a curved sausage shape. Note: the ends are rounded and stubby rather than pointed.
3. Dip a hooked piece of 28 gauge wire into Tylose glue.
4. Insert the wire into 1 end of the paste and allow to dry.
5. As soon as the bud has dried dust the curve with a little leaf green. Use white to lighten the green (mix lime with a hint of brown) so that it is very pale.

Snail Creeper

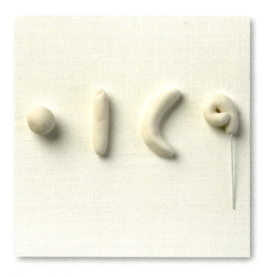

Large Buds

1. Take a much larger ball of white flower paste.
2. Make the ball of paste into a sausage shape with blunt ends.
3. Pinch a ridge along one side of the sausage of paste.
4. Curl the sausage of paste into a tight corkscrew shape.
5. Insert a piece of 24 gauge wire.
6. Allow the curled up bud to dry on bubble foam.

7. Dust the middle with a mix of rose and Barney and the underside of the bud with lilac, P pink, Barney and turquoise.
8. When all the different sizes have been made and dusted, spray lightly with confectioners glaze as in real life they have a waxy appearance.

Flower

1. Take a small piece of white flower paste the approximate size of a marble.
2. Form the ball into a cone shape.
3. Using your fingers pull the cone on 1 side to create a small sac with a tail.
4. Hollow out the sac and pull the tail into a corkscrew shape.
5. Insert a 24 gauge wire, with a small hook in the end, that has been moistened with Tylose glue.
6. Shape the edges of the little hat part. Trim and allow to dry.
7. Dust with lime and a little yellow mixed with cornflour. The tail is white with a little yellow on the tip.

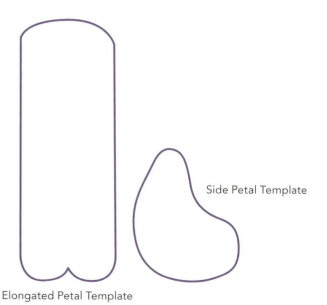

Side Petal Template

Elongated Petal Template

Artistic

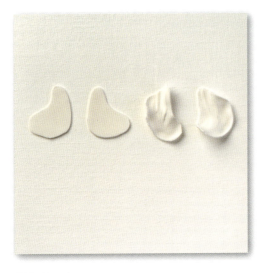

Side Petals

The petals curl back on themselves and each flower is different.

1. Roll out a piece of white flower paste.
2. Vein the petal well (a lily veiner will allow you to get good ridges in the petal).
3. Ball with a large balling tool to curl the outer edges so that they fold back and twist.
4. Dust the petals while they are damp with shades of magenta and purple by mixing these shades using colour guide reference.
5. Use Tylose glue to attach a petal on either side of the inner petal.

Elongated Petal

The last petal is an elongated, twisted petal.

1. Roll out a piece of white flower paste.
2. Cut out 1 petal using the template provided or use a cutter.
3. Ball the edges of the petal until the sides curl .
4. Fold the petal in half to create a centre vein.
5. Dust with a mix of yellow and lemon while still damp.
6. Attach the petal on the underside of the inner petal while still wet.
7. Twist the petal up onto itself into a corkscrew and allow to dry on bubble foam.

Assembly

The buds and flowers form in sprays. Tiny sprays form at the base of the small leaves and grow larger and larger in size as the creeper develops. The flowers grow in size, until they are almost 5cm, forming clumps of pretty, sweet smelling blooms.

1. Use a piece of 22 gauge wire.
2. Attach the smallest bud to the tip with a small thin piece of florist tape.
3. Tape several small buds to the top, 1 below each other and on opposite sides.
4. Slowly add bigger buds all the way down the stem until you get to the largest buds.
5. The open flowers form in a clump at the base of the stem.
6. The sprays form at the point where the leaves join the stem.

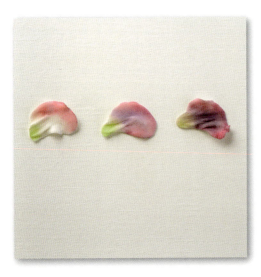

Leaves

The leaves start off very tiny in a close bunch at the tip of the stem.

When the leaves reach a certain size 1 side of the leaf broadens and flattens out.

Small Leaves

1. Roll a small piece of mid-green flower paste into a pea-sized ball.
2. Flatten and roll with a ridge down the middle.
3. Cut out 1 small leaf.
4. Insert a 28 gauge wire dipped in a little Tylose glue carefully into the thick part of the paste.
5. Lightly thin the edge with a small balling tool.
6. Press gently into a leaf former.
7. Allow to dry.
8. Dust with lime, yellow and a hint of brown mixed together.
9. Steam to set the colour and give the leaf a natural sheen.
10. Once the leaves are dry, wire them close together in a group of 3.

Large Leaves

1. Make the leaves in exactly the same manner as the small ones ensuring the centre of the leaf is thicker to accommodate a bigger wire.
2. The veins are well marked. Use a former (or dry a real leaf and use it to make the imprint).
3. Allow the leaf to dry flat as it does not curl.
4. Colour the top of the leaf a deeper shade of green by adding a hint more lime and brown and the underside a lighter green.
5. Once dry the leaves are wired together in the same group of 3.
6. Wire 2 leaves lower down on the sides.
7. Steam to set the colour and give a shiny gloss to the leaf.

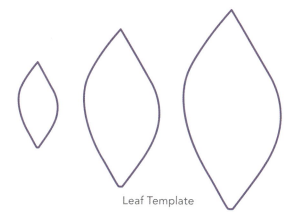

Leaf Template

Assembly

This creeper has long tendrils and grows climbing up walls and trees.

1. Take a 22 gauge wire taped in green florist tape.
2. Tape the smallest cluster of leaves at the top of the wire.
3. Wire the next set of leaves, slightly larger in size, lower down.
4. Wire the leaves to the main piece of 22 gauge wire all the way to the bottom ending with the largest set.
5. The set of 3 leaves has a piece of stem before attaching to the main stem so do not wire them too close together.
6. Once you have ended with the largest leaves, bend the stem into a natural curve as if it were a creeper.
7. The flower bunches start to develop where each set of leaves joins the main stem. Add small bunches of buds on some of the leaf tendrils where the smallest leaves join the main stem and full bunches with open flowers where you have attached the largest leaves.

Clivia

Stamens, Anther and Pistol

1. Cut 6 lengths of 28 gauge wire measuring 5cm and dust yellow.
2. Cut 1 longer piece of 24 gauge wire, 9cm in length to form the pistol, the bottom piece forms the stem of the flower.
3. Tape the stamens to the pistol with florist tape.
4. Each stamen has an anther secured to the top. To make the anther roll out a very tiny sausage of white flower paste. Paint the tip of the stamen with a little Tylose glue and secure the sausage shape. Dust yellow, then paint with a little Tylose glue and dip in yellow pollen.

The clivia is a member of the Amaryllidaceae family and is indigenous to Southern Africa, where they grow wild in forested areas. They are ideal for mass planting and make a great show when they flower. The flowers are formed in clusters on thick stems – a head can have as many as 20 flowers on it – and the colours range from deep orange to red and yellow. The leaves are strap shaped, fleshy and multiply prolifically, forming rich leafy cover under shady trees.

Materials

Flower paste

Powder colours: yellow, lemon, snow, lime, brown

Tylose glue

28, 26, 24 & 22 gauge wire

Fine 28 gauge wire

Clivia former

Florist tape

Modelling tools

Lifter

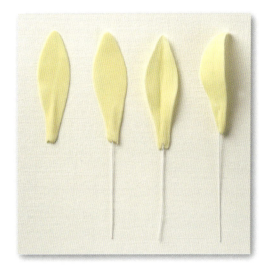  

3 Larger Petals

1. Use a small ball of lemon flower paste.
2. Roll out the paste using a grooved board or roll a ridge in the centre of the paste.
3. Cut out the larger petal shape.
4. Dip a ¼ length piece of 26 gauge wire into Tylose glue and then insert into thickened ridge area.
5. Ball the petal to thin the edges.
6. Vein lightly down the length of the petal with a veiner.
7. Place the petal onto the clivia former to give it a cupped shape.
8. Cut 2 more of the larger petals in the same manner and let all 3 petals stiffen slightly.
9. The petals can be dusted at this stage (or it can be left until the end). The base is light lime and pale yellow and the top of the petal is a deeper yellow colour.

Tip

If you do not have a Clivia former you can also use an Alstroemeria petal former to shape the top of the petals or pinch the top and allow to dry on bubble sponge.

3 Smaller Petals

1. Roll out a small piece of lemon flower paste.
2. Cut out 3 of the smaller petals without inserting wire. These form the outer petals.
3. Lie the first 3 wired petals onto a board.
4. Glue the very edges of the large petals ¾ of the way up.
5. Place the smaller petals between the large petals.
6. Use a roller lightly on the base to press them together firmly.
7. Carefully roll up the petals in a circle to form the flower and glue the edges of the petals together where they meet.

8. Pull the wired pistol and stamens through the centre of the flower.
9. Tape the flower together at the bottom with florist tape.
10. Shape the petals carefully and allow the flower to dry in a former.
11. Once the flower is dry, dust with very pale lime at the base of the flower and pale buttercup yellow to a brighter yellow at the top of the petals.

Note

Some of the varieties open up wide and others stay a bit more closed with the tips of the petals curving back slightly.

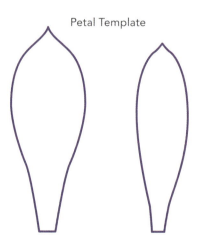 

Petal Template   Leaf Template

Buds

1. Use the same pale yellow paste for the larger buds as used for the flowers.
2. Make a hook in a ¼ length 24 gauge piece of wire and dip the end into Tylose glue.
3. Make a small sausage of yellow paste measuring 2cm in length.
4. Insert the piece of wire.
5. Work a piece of paste a few millimetres down the wire and form a little bulb at the base of the bud.
6. Using your fingers work the sausage of paste into a bud shape as shown. The very tip has a point to it but the top is slightly bulbous in shape.
7. Use a hat-pin or knife to make 3 even cuts into the bud from the bulb at the bottom to the tip of the bud.
8. Use a pair of tweezers to pinch a ridge ¾ of the way up alongside the grooves.
9. Allow to dry.

10. Dust the bud lime and lemon mixed together. The base of the bud is darker than the tip. Overdust the tip with yellow.
11. The larger the bud the more yellow it is in colour.

Leaves

The leaves are long, strappy looking and fleshy. They can look rather overpowering if placed on a cake, so it is acceptable to use a scaled down version using only the top half of the leaf.

1. Colour a piece of paste a mix of lime and hint of brown to achieve a medium to dark green.
2. Roll out the paste making sure it is not too thin as the leaf is fleshy.
3. Cut out 1 leaf shape. This can be done free hand or using the leaf template below.
4. Soften the edges with a balling tool.
5. Vein the leaf with a grooving tool or use a veiner.
6. Dry the leaf with a slight inward curve, remembering that the leaf should be very straight in shape and quite rigid.

 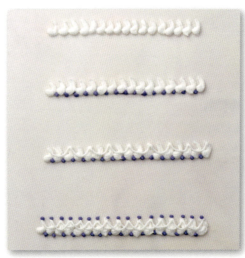 

Flowers

The flowers generally have 6 petals (newer hybrids have double petals), 6 stamens and a pistol. The anthers are yellow and covered with pollen.

Pods

The yellow Clivia produces seed pods which are quite large in size. They look like large dumpy berries and when they are ripe they often swell and split, with the seeds inside already sprouting roots. They have not been used in this arrangement.

Assembly

The flowers can be taped onto the thick strappy stem but, unless icing a botanical specimen, they are best arranged flower by flower. Display them in a group with a few leaves for best effect, as the stems are bulky and look heavy in an arrangement.

Decorative Work

Royal Icing Edging

The edge has been piped with royal icing using a small star nozzle.

1. Pipe a line of shelling along the base of the cake where it joins the board (base border). The shells tails curl upwards and are not piped straight.
2. Over pipe the shells with loops using a No. 0 writing tube.
3. Using a No. 0 writing tube and mauve royal icing mixed to medium peak pipe small dots along the top and bottom edges to finish the interesting design.

Colour Striping

To achieve the colour effect, add splotches of liquid colour to the ball of icing when rolling out the sugar paste. Knead lightly and roll with a rolling pin as you normally would when covering a cake. The colour will mix and form swirls as you roll it out, giving a marble effect.

Tip

Don't work the paste too much as the colours then become blurred into one and the marble effect will be lost.

Assembly

The unusual shape and design of this cake has been accomplished by cutting a large round cake diagonally to create two semi circles. The two tiers have been placed one on top of the other and the spray of flowers nestles comfortably where the tiers meet, forming a focal point in the design. The cake covering is sugarpaste which has been marbled by colour-striping the paste before rolling it out. A modern artistic look is achieved using this technique which complements the colours of the flowers in the spray. When using different colours, textures and shapes it is very important to ensure the design of the cake, the size of the board and the flower arrangement are in balance with each other so the arrangement is pleasing to the eye.

Cheerful

This cheerful cake, which showcases the delicate marguerite daisy, evokes feelings of joy. The rounded posy formation of the arrangement balances the straight horizontal and vertical dimensions of the cake.

The refreshing lemon and green tones make this modern design appropriate for use on any special occasion.

Marguerite Daisy

page 26

Marguerite Daisy

Centre

1. Mix a small amount of sugarpaste with Tylose powder to make a putty like paste.
2. Roll a pea-sized ball of white paste and measure against the centre circle of the daisy cutter. The paste ball should fit into the centre circle of the cutter and just slide through it.
3. Cut this ball of paste in ½ and form a round ball of paste.
4. Hook the end of a ¼ length 26 gauge wire and bend it over itself horizontally to form ½ a T shape.

Argyranthemum This daisy grows in the garden and flowers from May until August. It is a lovely flower and adaptable to many uses in sugar floral art from wedding and christening cakes to decorated cookies and cupcakes. It can also be used in piped work as well as in butter cream designs.

Materials

White flower paste

Sugarpaste

Powder colours: emerald, lemon, lime, turquoise, snow, silver, viridian

Yellow pollen

Tylose powder

Confectioners glaze

33 & 26 gauge wire

Daisy cutter from gerbera set (smallest cutter)

Daisy leaf cutter template

Large textured cell stick

Fine embroidery scissors

Modelling tools

Marguerite Daisy

5. Burn the end of the wire until it is white hot using a tealight candle then insert it into the ball of white paste. The heat crystalises the sugar and it adheres immediately. Leave to settle for a minute and then flatten the top by gently pressing down on a flat surface. Pinch the bottom to secure the base of the wire.

6. Hold the centre in 1 hand and, using fine embroidery scissors held at a right angle (90°), cut tiny snips all over the top surface. Snips should be a couple of mm deep and as fine as possible in width.

7. Dust with emerald powder colour mixed with a little lemon.

8. Paint the green surface with Tylose glue and then dip in yellow pollen. Leave to dry thoroughly.

Petals

1. Using white flower paste, roll out a small amount of paste tissue paper thin. Cut out 2 of the daisy cutter shapes. Make sure that there are no furry edges by exerting firm pressure on the cutter. If necessary turn the board upside down. Release the paste from the board and gently rub the paste against the cutter to release individual petals.

2. Place the 2 petals on a hard non-stick surface (rolling out board) and vein each individual petal with the textured end of the large cell stick by holding the cell stick parallel to the board and pushing down gently. A little cornflour may be used on the cell stick to prevent sticking.

3. Turn each petal upside down on a balling mat and use the small balling tool to ball each individual petal from the outer edge to the centre. This gives movement to the petals.

4. Turn over to the right side and using the rounded edge of the large cell stick make a deep impression into the centre. This makes the petals stand up a little and curve naturally.

5. With a flat ended soft dusting brush, dust the centre with a mixture of emerald and lemon mixed with cornflour.

6. For lemon daisies, mix lemon and snow powder colour together and dust the back and front of the petal.

7. Dust the under side of the dried centre with Tylose glue. Push the wired centre through the centre of the shaped petal, supporting the petals with cupped fingers, until they reach the glued area of the centre. Hold flower upside down and gently secure.

8. Squeeze together making sure the petals sit around the base well and there is no white showing from the centre.

9. Repeat the process with the second shaped petal.

10. Hang upside down to dry.

11. For buds, squeeze the petals closely together using a stroking movement.

Cheerful 27

Calyx

1. Make some lime green flower paste and roll between the fingers to form tiny, individual sausages approximately 1mm wide and 3-5mm long.
2. Paint the base of the dried flower with Tylose glue right around the central wire.
3. With angled tweezers pick up the tiny bracts one by one and place them in a circular formation to form the calyx.
4. Once all bracts are placed, gently squeeze the base between the fingers to neaten and secure the paste. Ease around the flower but don't secure the top half of the calyx. This gives a more natural look.

Leaves

1. Roll out light lime green flower paste and cut out 1 shape using the daisy leaf cutter template.
2. Cut ¼ length 33 gauge wire and insert the wire into the base of the leaf, extending it approximately ½ way up the stem by squeezing firmly between the thumb and forefinger and 'feeling' the wire upwards. It is advisable to dip fingers into a little cornflour to prevent the paste sticking and ripping.
3. Gently remove the fingers and peel the paste off sideways. If you peel off forwards the paste will rip from the inserted wire.
4. Vein against a general purpose leaf veiner.
5. Ball gently on a balling pad with the rounded edge of the small cell stick and place on bubble sponge.
6. Place on a double white tissue and dust with yellow and then lime and viridian all over. Dust the underside with a small amount of the same colour as the top but add a little turquoise and a hint of silver as the underside of the leaf has a silvery appearance.
7. Hold the wired leaf in a tissue and spray with a 50/50 mixture of isopropyl alcohol and concentrated confectioners glaze. The tissue will absorb the excess glaze.
8. Leave to dry on bubble sponge.

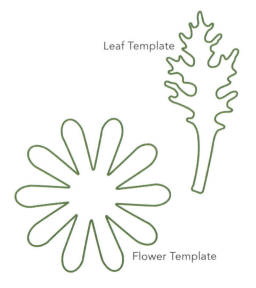

Assembly

The flowers have been wired into a delicate posy formation and placed on this classic square cake so that it resembles a present. Organza ribbon, overlaid with a simple contrasting satin ribbon, has been used to create this effect. A complementary 'dot' border and seed pearl stems complete the simple, yet stunning design.

Dramatic

This design is very dramatic. The black plate highlights the colours of the flowers and adds a 'zen-like' quality to the arrangement, which can be viewed from all angles. Although the arrangement is quite formal, it is also very unusual as it has no focal point. The flowers are grouped together to form a whole, with the different colours creating a dynamic contrast to each other. The bride who chose this design had a plate of flowers as a centrepiece on each table with all guests receiving a wrapped piece of cake on a miniature black plate to match.

Alstroemeria

Page 32

Wildfire hybrid tea rose

Page 35

Monstera Deliciosa

Page 39

Arum lily

Page 40

Forget-me-not

page 42

New Zealand flax

Page 44

Alstroemeria

Commonly called the Peruvian Lily or Lily of the Incas. This is a South American genus of about 50 flowering plants. Some are winter flowering and some are summer flowering plants, with many hybrids now evergreen and flowering for most of the year. The plants are found in many parts of the world. The plant flowers constantly and the flowers are popular with florists as they last well.

Materials

White flower paste
Powder colours: lilac, P pink, lime, Barney, snow, rubine, viridian, emerald
Tylose glue
28 & 24 gauge wire
Fine white stamens
Alstroemeria petal cutter or template
Alstroemeria former
Leaf cutter or template
Modelling tools

Stamens

There are 6 stamens and a stigma with the tip of the stigma divided into 3. Some stigmas are a pale brown in colour.

1. To form the pistol, remove the head from a cotton stamen.
2. Roll a little piece of paste onto the tip and cut into 3.
3. Tape a piece of 24 gauge wire about 5cm in length to the pistol.
4. Dip the tips of the stamens into gelatine powder which has been coloured pale yellow to form pollen.
5. Tape the stamens around the pistol making sure that they are slightly lower in height.
6. Dust the stamens and pistol a light lilac-pink by mixing lilac and P pink.

Petals

The flower has 6 petals – 3 are larger and cupped in shape, with the other 3 smaller and flatter in shape. The petals are well veined and each petal has a sharp tip, which is often green. The base of the petal is a pale lime/leaf green with the centre vein of the flower being darker than the outer edges.

1. Roll out a piece of white flower paste thinly, leaving a thicker piece in the middle. Alternatively use a grooved board.
2. Cut out 1 petal making sure the thicker ridge is in the middle of the petal.
3. Insert a piece of 28 gauge wire ⅓ of the way into the thickened part.
4. Ball the edges of the petal to thin and to give a slight curve to the petal.
5. Press into a petal former.
6. Allow to dry.
7. Cut 2 more petals and prepare in the same way.
8. Cut out 3 smaller petals in the same manner. These are not quite as curved but are also well veined.
9. Dust using a mix of P pink, lilac and a hint of Barney which have been blended to create the correct colour.
10. Place a larger petal onto a rolling board, then place a smaller petal on either side so they overlap the centre petal.
11. Flatten the base of the petals slightly with a roller to secure.
12. Tape the stamens to the 3 petals curving them naturally.
13. Tape the 2 larger petals on either side.
14. The last smaller petal sits between the 2 lateral petals and is slightly lower.

15. If the petals are not quite dry, pinch the bottom of the flower to neaten and tape securely with florist tape.
16. The bottom of the flower has a little veined knob. To make the knob wrap a small piece of light green paste around the bottom of the flower and pinch with tweezers to finish.
17. Allow the flower to dry completely, then steam to set the colour and give a natural shine.

Alstroemeria

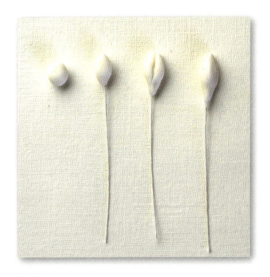

Buds

1. Start with a small marble of white flower paste.
2. Form the ball into a fat teardrop shape and insert a piece of 24 gauge wire.
3. Cut the tip of the bud into 3 and mark a deep vein into the bud following the line of each cut.
4. Pull each ⅓ of the bud into a slight ridge.
5. Shape with your fingers to neaten.
6. Allow to dry.
7. Using dusting powders, colour the base of the bud green using a lime and a touch of rubine. Colour the tip of the bud pale pink.
8. Make several sized buds from small to large.

Leaves

The leaves are elongated, medium green in colour and well veined. They twist slightly and bend.

1. Roll out a small piece of white flower paste using a grooved board.
2. Slip a 24 gauge wire into the ridge ⅓ of the way down the length of the leaf.
3. Ball the edges to thin.
4. Using a grooving tool, make veins down the length of the leaf.
5. Dust green using a little lime and emerald mixed together.
6. Spray with confectioner's glaze or steam well to create a natural shine.

Assembly

The stem has a number of leaves along its length interspersed with buds and flowers towards the top. Wire the leaves along the stem. Add buds and flowers to the main stalk, taping securely to form a flowering stem.

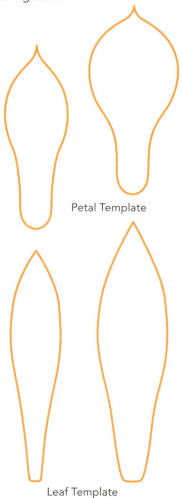

Petal Template

Leaf Template

Wildfire Hybrid Tea Rose

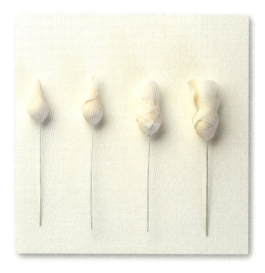

Cone
1. Take a marble-sized piece of white flower paste and roll into a smooth ball.
2. Roll the ball into a teardrop shape with the point at the top.
3. Make a hook in the end of a piece of 22 gauge wire. Dip into Tylose glue to moisten the hook and insert it into the base of the teardrop.
4. The cone should be ¾ the size of the largest cutter you are using.
5. Leave the cone to dry thoroughly.

Part of the Rosacece family, this orange coloured rose has fleshy petals which make it long lasting in a vase. The centre is burnt orange, with the outer petals slightly paler in colour. The reverse side is yellow. The buds, which are a pointed oval shape, are yellow with orange edges. The leaves are a semi-glossy, dark green.

Materials

White flower paste

Powder colours: yellow, lemon, orange, brown, viridian, lime, rubine, x red, snow, pearl lustre, x green

Tylose glue

28 & 22 gauge wire

Rose leaf cutters

Rose petal cutters

Rose veiner

Modelling tools

Paintbrush

4 teaspoons

Leaf Template

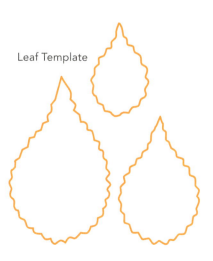

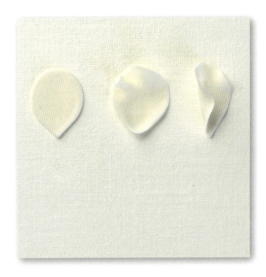
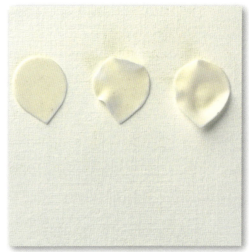
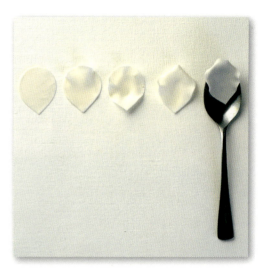

Flower

Only 3 sizes of petals were used to make this rose.

Petals (1st Row)

1. Cut out 2 of the smallest petals. Use a balling tool and a mat to ball out the petal, softening the edges so they are thin.
2. Vein using a rose petal veiner.
3. Moisten the cone slightly with a little Tylose glue and wrap the first petal around the tip of the cone.
4. The cone should not be seen at all so make sure that the first petal wraps tightly around the cone and sits higher than the top of the cone.
5. Ball out the second petal in the same manner.
6. Using a paintbrush moisten the first petal where it joins on the cone, only ½ way up from the base to approximately the middle.
7. Place the middle of the second petal on the join and wrap around, as with the first. They should both be the same height.

Petals (2nd Row)

1. Cut out 3 petals with the next size cutter.
2. Ball out the petals using a balling tool and vein using the rose petal veiner.
3. Moisten the very edge of each petal on the left hand side from the sharp tip at the bottom to ½ way up.
4. Place the middle of the first petal onto the cone where the join is.
5. Press down the glued edge.
6. Tuck the next 2 petals inside each other making sure it is the left hand side that is glued down.
7. The 3 petals for this rose are level with the first 2.
8. Curl the unglued side of each petal back slightly to create softness and movement.

Petals (3rd Row)

1. Using the biggest size cutter, cut out 4 petals.
2. Ball out the petals. The edges of the petals should be smooth, thin and cleanly cut.
3. Vein using the rose petal veiner.
4. Using 4 teaspoons, place each petal in a teaspoon then fold the very edge of the petal over the back of the spoon. This gives the petal a lovely shape and natural form. Allow to firm slightly.
5. Take the petals off the spoons and attach as before. These petals curve back and are also a lot looser, standing away from the cone.
6. Make sure the base of the cone is covered by the petals and is neat and tidy.

Petals (Last Row)

1. Roll out a piece of paste, thicker than for the previous petals.
2. Cut out 5 petals using the largest cutter. Ball well, stretching the paste so that the petals are bigger than the previous 4.
3. Vein using the rose petal veiner.
4. Place the petals onto the teaspoons. Curl the petals back over the spoon, particularly the sides, curving them so that the petal becomes almost pointed in shape. Make sure each petal has a good curve to it as the edge of this rose is soft and curved but not frilly.
5. When the petals are set but not dry attach them in the same manner as before. These petals are loose and stand back from the rose. They lie slightly lower than the others.
6. Allow the rose to dry well.

Colouring the Rose

This rose is a bright orange, with the centre a darker burnt orange. The reverse side of the petal is a pale yellow colour.

1. Once the rose is dry use a soft paintbrush, a little larger in size, and dust the reverse side of the rose petals with pale yellow and buttercup yellow (mix lemon and yellow). The base of the rose is the palest.
2. Use a small brush to carefully brush the petals in the centre of the rose.
3. Starting in the centre of the rose, carefully dust the petals with burnt orange by mixing a hint of x red and orange together. Add a little brown to achieve the correct shade.
4. The outer petals are a paler orange. Use snow petal dust to make the colour paler.

5. Petals can also be dusted when they are still soft, however the colours sometimes tend to streak if not well blended prior to dusting, so it is preferable to colour when the rose is dry.
6. Steam lightly over a boiling kettle to set the colour.

Calyx

The size of the calyx is important – it should fit the base of the rose adequately, with the tips long enough to curl back on an open rose.

1. Roll a small marble-sized piece of paste into a smooth round ball.
2. Shape the ball of paste into a teardrop shape.
3. Flatten the base of the teardrop to form a Mexican hat shape.
4. Place the calyx cutter over the Mexican hat and cut out one calyx. The balance should be correct.
5. Use a balling tool on a petal pad to stretch out the sepals and thin the edges.
6. Cut the edges of each sepal with a fine pair of scissors to create little sliced indents.
7. Use a small cell stick to hollow out the centre of the Mexican hat.
8. Colour the calyx with viridian and use a little light brown on the edges of the sepals.

9. The inside of the calyx is paler so use a little pearl lustre mixed with lemon dust to create a natural effect.
10. Wet the hollow with a little Tylose glue and slide the wired rose through the centre.
11. Make sure the sepals cover the joins between the petals. Secure with a little Tylose glue.
12. Use your fingers to create the small bulge at the base of the rose calyx. This later forms the rose hip.
13. Make sure the calyx is secured and the sepals evenly spaced.

Calyx Template

Petal Template

  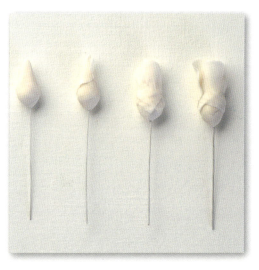

Leaves

The rose has a large leaf at the apex, then 2 medium leaves lower down. The last 2 are the smallest.

1. Colour white flower paste a pale green (x green is a good base colour to use).
2. Roll out a piece of flower paste with a ridge in the centre. Alternatively use a grooved board.
3. Cut out 1 leaf using a rose leaf cutter.
4. Insert a moistened piece of thin 28 gauge wire.
5. Ball the edges of the leaf to thin and soften. Allow the edges to curl slightly as it gives movement to the leaf.
6. Vein the leaf and allow to dry on bubble foam.
7. Cut out 5 leaves in total – 1 large, 2 medium and 2 small – in the same manner.

Colouring the Leaves

1. Dust the leaves with viridian, lime and x green.
2. Use a mix of pearl lustre, lime and viridian to create a pale underside.
3. The leaves have a hint of pink on the edges. Use a flat paintbrush to apply a little rubine dusting powder to the very edges of the leaf.
4. Steam well and spray with confectioners glaze to create a natural gloss.
5. Tape the leaves together – the largest at the top, 2 medium leaves lower down in a pair and lastly the pair of 2 small leaves.
6. Tape the leaves onto the rose stem with buds.
7. Colour the stems for the leaves and the main stem with a little viridian green and a little rubine where the leaves meet so that the spray looks life-like.

Buds

1. The bud is made using a cone, the same size as the large rose.
2. The first two rows of petals are made and attached in the same manner. Soften the edges of the petals and vein. Ball the petals in the centre so that they are cupped.
3. Use the largest petal cutter of the 3. Roll out 3 petals.
4. Ball out each petal and vein. Fold the petals back around the edges.
5. Glue onto the cone in a spiral as with a full rose but cup the petals closer to form a bud shape.
6. Make sure the bottom of the cone is covered and neat.
7. Colour the bud with the same burnt orange shade.
8. Attach a calyx so that the sepals reach the tip of the bud.
9. Allow to dry and then steam lightly to set the colour.

Monstera Deliciosa

Also called Swiss Cheese plant or Delicious Monster, this plant is a creeping vine which originated in the tropical rainforests of Southern Mexico to Panama. It has a thick stem and large, leathery heart-shaped leaves which are used by florists as they are a lovely, glossy green. The leaf has a natural curve but lies fairly straight. The colour of the leaf is evenly toned and the underside is a much paler green. When they are young the leaves are pale green and furled like a flag.

Materials

White flower paste

Powder colours: viridian, lime, brown

Tylose glue

Confectioners glaze

24 gauge wire

Modelling tools

Leaves

1. Colour a golf ball-sized piece of paste a medium lime colour.
2. Roll out a good size piece of paste on a grooving board – the thickened groove needs to be in the middle of the leaf.
3. Cut out 1 leaf and insert a 24 gauge wire that has been dipped in Tylose glue.
4. Ball edges on a petal pad and fold the leaf in half to create a central vein. Use a former to vein the leaf. You can also use a cell pin to vein from the main centre vein to the outer edge of the leaf, following the 'leaf fingers'.
5. Allow the leaf to dry with a natural curve then dust with a mix of viridian, lime and a little brown.
6. Steam over a boiling kettle to set the colour and allow to dry.
7. Spray with confectioners glaze to gloss.

Arum Lily

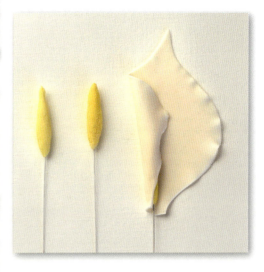

Zandtedeschia Aethiopica *The genus is restricted to the African continent. It is evergreen, or deciduous, depending on habitat and rainfall. The Arum comes in many colours from pinks and yellow to a dark crimson and greens, however, the most common is the white Arum. It is a popular flower with modern brides.*

The Arum has a yellow spadix which is surrounded by a white or coloured spathe, although the spathe is in fact a modified leaf and not a flower.

Materials

Flower paste

Powder colours: lime, viridian, rubine, rose, x red, yellow

Tylose glue

Gelatine (coloured yellow for pollen)

Arum cutters or template

22 gauge wire

Lily veiner

Modelling tools

Spadix

These can be made ahead of time and left.

1. Colour a small ball of sugar paste mid-yellow.
2. Make a hook in a piece of 22 gauge wire.
3. Take a small marble-size piece of paste and roll it into a fat worm shape.
4. Form the top end into more of a point.
5. Roll the piece about 5cm in length. The length of the spadix is $\frac{2}{3}$ that of the cutter length.
6. Dip the hooked 22 gauge wire in Tylose glue and insert into the roll of paste $\frac{3}{4}$ of the way.
7. Dip into coloured gelatine or 'pollen'.
8. Allow to dry.

Spathe

The spathe curls around the spadix in either direction, left or right. The buds and young flowers are more tightly curled and the older the flower (which is in fact a modified leaf) the more open it is. As the flower ages the spathe becomes greener. The stem is thick and fleshy.

1. Roll out a piece of white flower paste.
2. Cut out a spathe shape.
3. Ball the edges to thin and create a curly edge.
4. Moisten the base of the spathe with Tylose glue.
5. Wrap the spathe around the spadix.
6. Curl back the long edge that overlaps.
7. The point at the top is pinched and also curls back a little.
8. Hang the lily upside down.
9. Allow to dry.
10. Using dusting powders colour the flower a mix of rubine and rose using a flat-ended paintbrush. The flower is streaky with green at the base and on the tip of the spathe. Dust with a hint of lime mixed with cornflour.
11. Steam the flower to set the colour.
12. Tape the wire with pale green florist tape a few times to thicken.

Tips

In this design the Arums are used in a tight modern arrangement and therefore the leaves have not been included as they are rather large and fleshy. Bunched together they look eye-catching and add form and line to an arrangement.

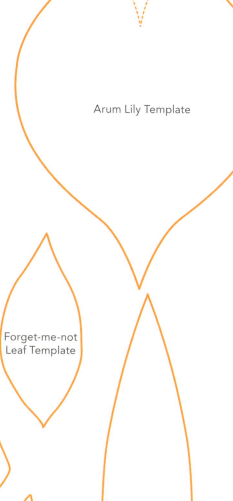

Arum Lily Template

Forget-me-not Leaf Template

New Zealand Flax Template

Forget-me-not Flower Template

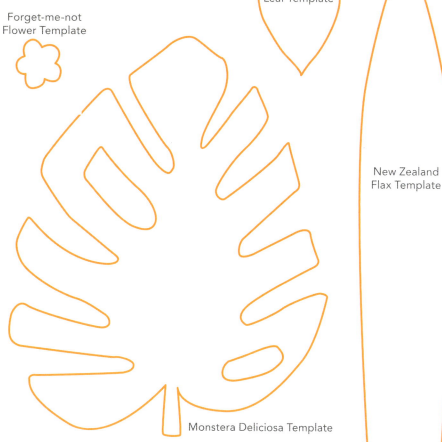

Monstera Deliciosa Template

Forget-me-not

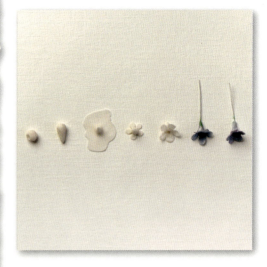

Duranta Erecta, Family Verbenaceae
Commonly known as the Forget-me-not tree. This large shrub, which can grow big enough to be considered a tree, originated in the tropical areas of America. It has clusters of bright yellow/orange berries that follow after the flowers have dropped. The small lavender-blue flowers appear in loose clusters and have two little dark blue stripes on the lower petals. The flowers are very pretty and have a vanilla smell. The foliage is usually a yellow, leafy green or variegated.

Materials

Flower paste

Powder colours: lime, yellow, orange, blue, lilac, Barney, turquoise, viridian, brown

Liquid colour: blue mixed with Barney

Tylose glue

30, 28 & 24 gauge wire or stamens

Fine paintbrush

Hat-pin

Modelling tools

Flowers

1. Colour a small quantity of flower paste a lavender/pale blue by mixing a little lilac and a hint of Barney and turquoise.
2. Roll a small piece of paste into a tiny ball.
3. Form the ball of paste into a cone or teardrop shape.
4. Flatten the base of the teardrop.
5. Roll the paste out thinly around the apex of the teardrop.
6. Place the cutter over the top of the cone and cut out 1 flower.
7. Create a hollow in the centre of the flower with a small cell stick.
8. Ball out the petals using a small balling tool – the front 2 bottom petals curl back slightly.
9. Use a hat-pin to make 1 little groove on the 2 bottom petals, from the centre to the outer petal.
10. Pull a stamen through the centre of the flower. Or use a piece of 30 gauge wire with a small hook at the top. Wet the hook or stamen head with Tylose glue before inserting.
11. Finish off the base of the flower neatly forming the calyx. The flower should be slightly elongated.
12. Use a very fine paintbrush to colour the little groove with blue liquid colouring.
13. Allow to dry.
14. Make a number of the small flowers as each spray has several buds and flowers on the stalk.

Buds

The buds are very small. The bottom of the bud is coloured green and the tip is blue. The larger buds have a bigger bulge at the top and slant slightly.

1. Use a tiny piece of flower paste to start.
2. Roll the paste into a small teardrop shape.
3. Wet the tip of a stamen with Tylose glue.
4. Insert the stamen into the teardrop.
5. Shape into a little cone-shaped bud.
6. Colour the bottom lime and the tip a hint of blue.
7. Make several buds and allow to dry.

Leaves

The leaves are straight along the edges with a central vein. They range from light to dark green and change to yellow/green with age.

1. Use a marble size ball of pale lime flower paste.
2. Roll out paste on a grooved board.
3. Cut out 1 leaf using a cutter or template. Note: the thick ridge needs to be in the centre of the leaf.
4. Damp a 28 gauge wire with Tylose glue and insert into the thick part of the leaf.
5. Ball the edges to thin.
6. Fold the leaf in half to create a crease.
7. Place into a leaf veiner and allow to dry.
8. Dust the leaf with viridian and a little lime. Dust the underside with a mixture of lime and brown.
9. Steam to create a gloss.
10. Make several sized leaves – from small to large.

Berries

The berries are green when tiny and develop a bright yellow/orange colour as they ripen. They form exactly where the flowers drop off.

1. Roll a little ball of yellow/orange paste.
2. Damp the tip of a stamen with a little Tylose glue and insert the stamen into the little ball of paste.
3. Sharpen the end of the ball.
4. Allow to dry.
5. Dust with yellow and orange dusting powder.
6. Colour the tip of the berry with a little lime.
7. Attach the berries in pairs on a piece of wire to form a spray.

Assembly

1. Use a 24 gauge wire to form the centre stalk.
2. Attach the buds neatly with thin pieces of florist tape.
3. Start with the smallest bud at the top.
4. Place all the buds along the stem.
5. Bend the buds upright so that they stand vertical to the stem
6. Add the flowers to the stem after the largest bud.
7. The leaves are then attached to the end of the stem.
8. Form small bunches of the flowers and berries, both of which are found on the shrub at the same time.

New Zealand Flax

Phormium *Originated in New Zealand. These plants have either green or bronze colouring and some varieties can grow to a height of a several metres. New Zealand flax are used as landscaping plants in gardens and are a favourite with florists as they can be rolled or wired into different shapes.*

Materials

White flower paste

Light green/lime flower paste

Powder colour: lime

Modelling tools

Leaves

The leaves are generally very straight, so care needs to be taken in shaping them so they do not look lifeless.

1. Roll 2 marble size pieces of white flower paste.
2. Roll 1 marble size ball of light lime paste.
3. Form the balls into sausage shapes.
4. Flatten each sausage of paste into a strip using a small roller.
5. Merge the 3 strips together side by side with the green strip in the middle and the 2 white strips on either side.
6. Make sure the white strips overlap the edges of the green strip slightly.
7. Roll the strips lengthways. Apply even pressure to keep the lines as straight as possible.
8. Cut out a leaf shape using a cutter, template or free hand.
9. Use a grooving tool to create veins down the length of the leaf.
10. Fold the leaf in half to form a clear central vein.
11. Allow the leaf to dry.
12. Touch up the green with a little lime dusting powder to give life to the leaf.
13. The leaf can be rolled to give interest to an arrangement, or left straight and used to give shape and line.

Assembly

The black plate acts as a dramatic backdrop to the colourful flowers. As the design has no focal point, the flowers have been carefully sized in order for the arrangement to be balanced. The different leaves give form and shape and act as a green foil for the coloured flowers.

The largest flowers are the arums, grouped together on one side of the plate. The roses are centered and raised to give height to the arrangement and the mauve shading of the alstoemeria complements the orange roses. The different shapes of the flowers add interest, while the small berries look very natural hanging over the edge of the plate.

Elegant

This elegant cake has an air of peace and tranquility.
The monochromatic colour theme creates elegance and style while
the understated arrangement of cherry blossom and
lace flowers gives a feeling of the Orient.

Indian hawthorn has been used as a central focal point to maintain
harmony in the design.

Flowering plum

page 48

Indian hawthorn

page 52

Lace flowers

page 55

Flowering Plum

Leaf

1. Roll out a piece of white flower paste very thinly.
2. Cut out 1 large, 2 small and 2 medium leaf shapes.
3. Cut ¼ length 33 gauge wire. Dip fingers into cornflour (this prevents sticking) and insert the wire into the paste by exerting firm pressure and feeling the wire approximately 1.5cm up the centre of the leaf.
4. Peel the leaf sideways from the fingers so the wire does not come through the paste.
5. Vein on a rose leaf veiner.

Prunus Nigra or Rosaceae This is an ornamental flowering plum, native to North America, bearing deep purple foliage. It has a spectacular show in spring and bears pink/white flowers with ornamental fruits. The fruit are reddish in colour and shaped like small cherries. The fruit can be eaten raw or made into preserves or jellies.

Materials

White flower paste

Powder colours: rose, rubine, lime, lemon, brown, violet, x red

Confectioners glaze

Cornflour

Isopropyl alcohol

33 & 28 gauge wire

Superfine white stamens

Rose leaf cutters

Blossom cutters – medium and small

Brown florist tape

Rose leaf veiner or real rose leaf

Balling mat

Bubble sponge

Modelling tools

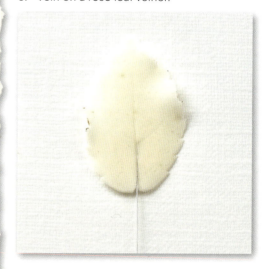

6. Place on a balling mat and thin the edges by placing the balling tool halfway on the paste and halfway off the paste exerting medium pressure to give the leaf movement.
7. Place on a double white tissue and dust both sides of the leaf with a 50/50 mixture of brown and rubine and a hint of violet. Blend all colours well with a flat-ended paintbrush.
8. Re-ball on the palm of the hand if necessary.
9. Slightly pinch the tip of the leaf and then bend it vertically in half so that it cups upwards slightly.
10. Dip and spin in a 50/50 mixture of confectioners glaze and isopropyl alcohol.
11. Hang upside down or lay on bubble sponge to dry.
12. Tape each leaf with ¼ width brown florist tape.

Assembly of Leaf

1. The leaves grow alternatively. Take 1 large leaf and gently curve the stem between the thumb and forefinger to give it a slightly natural shape.
2. Tape 4-5cm down the stem with brown florist tape.
3. Add 1 medium leaf, which has been given the same natural curve, to the right and add another on the opposite side and a little further down to the left.
4. Repeat the process for the small leaves.

Tips

- Always mix the colours together well with a flat-ended paintbrush on a double white tissue. This prevents colour speckles showing in the final dusted product.
- Prior to dipping in the glaze solution re-ball the edges of the petal firmly on the hand. This gives a shinier look to the edges after the glazing process.
- Make sure when veining that the central vein and the wire in the leaf are at the same point on the veiner.
- Remove all excess dusting powder before glazing as this will result in a cleanly shaded leaf.

Cherry Blossom Template

Leaf Template

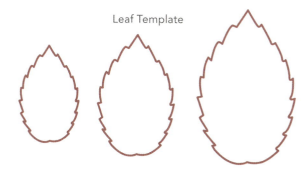

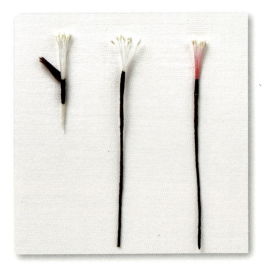  

Cherry Blossom

1. Cut 8 super fine stamens in ½. Tape the 16 stamens onto ¼ length 33 gauge wire using ¼ width brown florist tape. Leave 1cm of stamen exposed.
2. Dust the base with rose.
3. Dust the tips with lemon powder colour and slightly overdust with a hint of lime (use the excess lime which has been left on your green dusting brush). The anther is barely green with a lot of lemon showing through.
4. Spread the stamens in a fan-like formation.
5. Cut 2 large blossoms out of white flower paste.
6. Vein on a rose petal veiner.
7. Ball on a balling mat to thin the edges.
8. Place on the hard rolling board and roll each petal from the left to right with the pointed end of the small cell stick. This gives the flower a natural look.
9. Cut out 1 smaller blossom and repeat the process.
10. Place the 2 large petals on top of one another and in-between one another and then do the same with the smaller ones. Secure the individual petals with a hint of Tylose glue.

Flowering Plum

11. Place the petals on the balling mat and indent the middle with the rounded edge of a large cell stick. This will cup the petals.
12. Paint the base of the stamens where the taping begins with a little Tylose glue and place the wire in the middle of the flower and feed through.
13. Pinch the base of the flower paste to secure the flower to the stamens.
14. Hang upside down to dry.

Assembly
- There is a particular pattern to the cherry blossoms however they tend to grow in a cluster formation.
- Prunus cherry blossoms can be single or double blossoms.
- To give a huge impact randomly tape them in between the prunus leaves.

Tip

Although the blossoms have a pink appearance it is not necessary to shade the paste pink as the centre pink of the stamens gives a gentle hue to the petals.

Fruit

The fruits are fleshy and measure 2cm long (but are scaled down a little in size for cake decorating).

1. Cut ¼ length 28 gauge wire and hook the ends.
2. Roll small 1cm diameter balls of white paste.
3. Paint the ends of the wire with a little Tylose glue and insert into the balls of paste.
4. Roll slightly on a balling mat to slightly elongate the fruit and then pinch the base.
5. Mark a central line down 1 side only using a trowel or cutting blade.
6. Dust with rubine and x red mixed with a little brown and violet.
7. Steam to set the colour by waiving the cherries over the steam of a kettle or boiling pot of water.
8. Tape the stem with brown florist tape and then overdust with the same red shade.
9. Dip and spin in confectioners glaze and hang upside down to dry.

Note

Although the fruit is described it has not been used on this cake.

Indian Hawthorn

Centre

1. Cut 5 superfine stamens in ½. Leave 1cm exposed and then tape 10 stamens to 33 gauge wire using green florist tape.
2. Dust the base with a 50/50 mixture of rubine and rose.
3. Mix a little brown petal dust with isopropyl alcohol and paint the tips of the stamens.
4. Run your finger over the top of the bunch of stamens to spread them outwards.

Raphiolepus Indica This plant is a genus of the rose family and is attractive to bees, birds and butterflies. The branches bear clusters of white massed flowers and buds tapering down the stem and surrounded with waxy, dark green leaves, which have serrated edges. It bears tiny purplish-black berries after it has flowered and is an attractive flower when used in sugar art. The only part of the plant used in this cake is the flower.

Materials

Flower paste

Powder colours: rubine, rose, P pink, lemon, lime, brown, violet, blue

Cornflour

Tylose glue

Isopropyl alcohol

Confectioners glaze

Petal base

33 & 28 gauge wire

Superfine white stamens

5 petal blossom cutter

Small star cutter

General purpose leaf veiner

Mid-green florist tape

Modelling tools & balling mat

Flower Template   Calyx Template

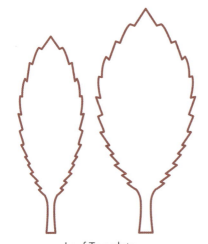

Leaf Template

Flower

When the flowers are young the centre stamens are green and as the flower ages they become a deep purple shade.

1. Take a small pea-sized ball of white paste and shape into a witch's hat.
2. Stretch the flower paste outwards with the end of a paintbrush.

3. Cut out 1 blossom shape from the witch's hat.
4. Press the petal edges between the fingers and then place on a balling mat and stretch outwards using the small balling tool.
5. Hollow the centre with the pointed end of a small cell stick which has been dipped in cornflour to prevent sticking.
6. Turn the flower over – flat side down – on a balling pad.
7. With small cell stick, gently stretch the petals sideways.
8. Paint the base of the stamens where the colour starts with a little Tylose glue.
9. The stamens should protrude from the flower only a little (1cm).
10. Place the centre stamens down the middle of the hawthorn blossom and squeeze gently to secure. Roll between the thumb and forefinger to thin the paste stem.

Note

The flowers are slightly serrated on the edges.

Flower Calyx

1. Colour a small piece of flower paste mid-green.
2. Form into the shape of a witch's hat.
3. Roll out paste extremely thinly and cut out 1 calyx shape.
4. Thin the edges of the bracts with a small balling tool and paint the centre with a little Tylose glue.
5. Place the flower through the middle of the formed calyx and secure.
6. The calyx sits flush with the flower and does not bend backwards.
7. Dust the calyx with a little lime and lemon mixed together.

Buds

1. Cut a 33 gauge wire ¼ length and hook the end.
2. Roll out a glass pinhead-sized ball of white flower paste.
3. Paint the hooked wire with a little Tylose glue.
4. Secure the ball of paste on the hooked wire by gently rolling a little way down the stem.
5. Pinch the tip of the bud so it comes to a point.
6. Make the calyx for the bud in exactly the same manner as the flower calyx was made.
7. Make many buds in varying sizes, with the largest being the glass pinhead-sized bud.
8. Dust the calyx with a little lime powder colour mixed with lemon.

Leaves

Leaves vary in size and have serrated edges.

1. Roll out light green flower paste thinly and cut out 1 leaf shape.
2. Cut ¼ length 33 gauge wire.
3. Dip fingers in cornflour and insert the wire from the base ⅓ of the way up using firm pressure between the thumb and the forefinger.
4. Peel the leaf off the finger sideways (do not peel from the top as the wire will rip the paste).
5. Place the upper side of the leaf on a general purpose leaf veiner and press down firmly with a small sponge to vein.
6. Lay the leaf on the balling mat and thin the edges gently to give movement.
7. Place on a double white tissue and dust with yellow and then lime. Overdust with viridian for a deeper green shade.
8. Dip the leaf in a 50/50 mixture of isopropyl alcohol and confectioners glaze. Let the excess drip off the leaf and then leave it to dry, hanging it upside down on a petal dryer.
9. Tape the stem with mid-green florist tape.

Assembly of Flowers, Buds and Leaves

1. Using mid-green florist tape, tape flowers and buds randomly downwards for the first 5cm in a staggered cluster-like formation.
2. Randomly tape leaves in varying sizes down the stem – there is no particular pattern.

Berries

1. Cut ¼ length 28 gauge wire and hook the end.
2. Roll a pea-sized ball of white flower paste.
3. Paint the tip of the hooked wire with Tylose glue. Insert into the ball of paste – let it protrude a little – and leave to dry.
4. Using the sharp end of a cell stick, indent the top of the berry slightly and then pinch a circle all the way around it.
5. Dust the berry all over with a mixture of violet and cornflour mixed with a hint of blue.
6. Steam to set the colour and then, while slightly moist, scatter a little Tylose powder over the berry.
7. When the berry is dried, a little darker violet can be blushed over 1 cheek of the berry. The berries are taped in the same manner as the flowers and buds.

Note

The berries are described but not included in the arrangement.

Lace Flowers

Lace flowers can be used as a central focal feature or in combination with any other complementary designs and give a lovely finishing touch to any cake.

Materials

2 tbsp stiff peak royal icing (refer royal icing section)
Extra sifted icing sugar
Powder colour: Snow
1 tbsp Tylose powder
4 tsp boiling water
Vegetable fat
Acetate paper
Piece of glass or Perspex
Traced flower templates
Writing tube No. 1
Piping bag
Trowel

Method

1. Mix Tylose powder with boiling water.
2. Let it form a gum glue and leave to stand for a couple of hours.
3. Add ½ tsp snow powder colour.
4. Mix in royal icing.
5. Add more sifted icing sugar until a medium peak consistency is achieved.
6. Fill piping bag with royal icing.
7. Place templates underneath a sheet of Perspex or glass.
8. Smear vegetable fat over the top of the glass.
9. Place acetate paper over the fat.
10. Pipe lace flower designs and allow to semi-dry.
11. Pick up the acetate paper and lay it against the side of the cake where the lace flower will be positioned.
12. Let all pieces dry thoroughly.
13. Remove the piping from the acetate paper by gently peeling away the paper from the piped work.

Lace Flowers

14. Secure the largest flower onto the cake with a little royal icing and then place the remaining piped layers on top of one another in the same way from largest to smallest.
15. Using artistic license place modelled Indian Hawthorn in the centre of the flower.

Tips
- Adding the Tylose powder to the royal icing makes the piped pieces a lot stronger and easier to assemble.
- You can pipe with a mixture of the Tylose powder, snow and water alone but the flowers often become too flexible and lose their shape easily.

Lace Flower Template

Assembly

The individual cakes have been covered with sugarpaste
and dusted with pearl lustre to give a light and reflective look.

A snail trail border has been piped to seal the joins and to present a professional overall finish.

Lace flowers complete the design and add to the cool theme.

They are secured to the cake using a little royal icing.

Exotic

This modern two-tier oval stacked cake combines a lively lime covering with a spirited arrangement of exotic blooms.

Double-crested tropical hibiscus and cerise pink frangipanis, together with hot pink mini gem anthiriums, create a colourful focal point, while the simple white bougainvillea balances the beauty of the arrangement.

This bright and breezy design would be perfect for a tropical celebration or beach wedding.

Hibiscus
page 60

Bougainvillea
page 64

Anthurium
page 66

Frangipani
page 69

Extension and Bridge work
page 72

Hibiscus

Centre
1. Cut ⅓ length 24 gauge wire.
2. Take 5 fine white stamens. Leave 2cm above the rounded end and tape them onto the 24 gauge wire using ¼ width fawn florist tape.
3. Dust the tips with rubine and apricot mixed together.
4. Dust a little apricot down the filament.
5. Take 5 superfine seed head stamens and dust them apricot. Tape them in from the commencement of the previous taping. Leave them all to one side.

Nicknamed 'Queen of the Tropics' this plant is also known as the Chinese or Hawaiian hibiscus. The double-crested hibiscus is widely grown throughout the tropics and sub tropics and there are approximately 250 species. Flowers vary from 7-25cm in diameter, depending on the species and come in a dazzling variety of shades, which include all of the colours in the colour chart – there are few flowers which sport this.

Materials

White and light green flower paste

Powder colours: lemon, apricot, peach, rubine, lime, yellow, flesh

33 & 24 gauge wire

White fine and superfine stamens

Double hibiscus cutters (refer templates)

Hibiscus leaf veiner

Large poppy veiner

Fawn and mid-green florist tape

Modelling tools

Large and small cell sticks

Bubble sponge

White tissues

  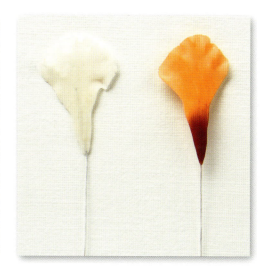

Flower Petals
Petaloids (1st Row)

1. Using the smallest cutter cut out 5 petals in thin white flower paste.
2. Vein with the large poppy veiner.
3. Frill the edges with a small cell stick.
4. Dust on a double white tissue with apricot powder colour using a flat soft-ended dusting brush.
5. Using the rounded end of the small cell stick ball from the base towards the middle of the petal on the palm of the hand.
6. Paint the base with a little Tylose glue.
7. Hold the wired stamens upside down between the thumb and the forefinger and wrap 1 petaloid around the centre stamens leaving 1cm of the tip exposed.

8. Wrap the second petal, working from left to right, and continue doing the same with the remaining petals.
9. Squeeze the base and twist between the fingers to secure.
10. Hang upside down to dry.
11. When completely dry, use a fine-ended brush to dust the inner base area with a little rubine powder colour mixed with apricot.

Middle Petals (2nd Row)

1. Cut ⅓ length 33 gauge wire.
2. Roll a small pea-sized ball of white flower paste firmly between the hands (ensuring all cracks and weak points are removed).
3. Moisten the wire with a little Tylose glue and insert into the ball of paste.
4. Form the paste into a teardrop shape ensuring that the tip of the wire stays ⅓ from the tip of the paste.
5. Flatten the teardrop with the forefinger by pressing down firmly on a hard surface.
6. Stretch the top ⅓ horizontally to form a fan-like shape. If cracks appear along the top this is good as this is how the petal is in nature. The thinner and more cracked the better.

7. Vein using the middle of the large poppy veiner.
8. Gently flute the top edge of the petal and give the shaft a gentle curve forwards.
9. Repeat another 7 times. Specimens vary in petal numbers but this example has 8 middle petals in total.
10. Shade all the petals apricot and then overdust with lemon and finally a touch of peach. Shading is done on a double white tissue using a flat soft-ended dusting brush.
11. For the finishing touch, shade the base and 5mm from the base of the petal a mixture of rubine and rose.

Base Petals (3rd Row)

1. Cut 5 x ⅓ lengths 33 gauge wire.
2. Roll out a piece of white flower paste very thinly and cut out 2 of the larger petal shapes.
3. Place the wire ⅔ of the way up the petal and secure with Tylose glue.
4. Place the second petal over the first petal and secure with a gentle stroke of the finger.
5. Place the small cell stick parallel to the central wire and thin either side of the wire. Re-cut with the same size cutter. Squeeze the base and roll between the fingers to secure the paste to the wire.

Assembly of the Flower

Calyx

6. Stretch the upper ⅓ of the petal outwards and sideways using the large cell stick.
7. Vein in the centre of the large poppy veiner.
8. Gently frill the top of the petal with a small cell stick. Again, should the paste crack, this is good as the real petals are jagged and cracked.
9. Dust with the same colours as the middle petals. The bottom half is dusted with rose and rubine mixed together.
10. Gently curve the bottom ⅓ upwards and leave to dry.

1. Tape in the first 4 petals of the second size petal evenly around the stamen with ¼ width fawn florist tape starting 1.5cm below the petaloids ensuring that the bases meet exactly.
2. Tape 5mm further down the staminal column (filament) and tape the remaining 4 petals in between the previously taped petals.
3. For the largest petals and the third row, tape 2cm down the staminal column and then tape in the remaining 5 petals.
4. Adjust the petals where necessary.

1. Mix a little lime flower paste.
2. Roll out a piece of paste very thinly and cut out 1 'crown' shape.
3. Vein on the top area of the large poppy veiner.
4. Thin the edges on a balling mat using the rounded side of a large cell stick.
5. Paint a strip of Tylose glue along the base of the crown and wrap the crown calyx shape around the flower ensuring that the edges meet.
6. Roll out another piece of green paste and cut out the second calyx (smaller star) bract shape.
7. Thin the edges and mark a central vein down the middle of each bract.
8. Pinch the tips between the fingers to give a pointed end.
9. Paint the middle with a little Tylose glue and attach to the base of the first 'crown' bract.
10. Dust the bottom with yellow powder colour.
11. Over-tape the staminal column with mid-green florist tape from the calyx to the bottom of the wire.

Leaves

1. Cut a ⅓ length 24 gauge wire.
2. Roll out a piece of light green flower paste very thinly on a grooved board.
3. Cut out 1 leaf shape.
4. Insert the wire into the leaf while it is still on the board pressing down firmly on the ridge as you are inserting the paste.
5. Vein using the hibiscus leaf veiner and thin the edges on a balling mat using the round end of the large cell stick.
6. Dust with yellow and overdust areas in lime.
7. Some leaves have variegated white spots on their leaves.
8. Spray the leaves with a confectioners glaze mix and leave to dry on bubble sponge.
9. Tape the stem with mid-green florist tape.

Buds

The buds vary in size depending on their growth stage.

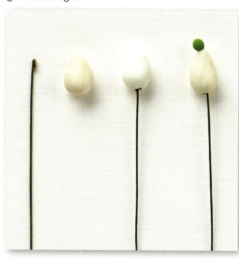

1. Roll a 7mm diameter ball of white paste. Leave the bottom rounded and place the forefinger approximately half way up the ball. Gently roll to thin and form a rounded point in the shape of a cone.
2. Burn a hooked 24 gauge wire into the cone. The heat crystalises the sugar and it adheres immediately.
3. Roll out a pinhead-sized ball of green flower paste.
4. Paint the top of the cone with Tylose glue and attach the ball. Leave to dry.
5. Roll green flower paste thinly and cut out 2 calyx shapes.
6. Vein each bract down the middle using the Dresden tool.
7. Place 1 on top of the cone and pinch the tip. Paint the underside of the bracts with Tylose glue to secure and pinch the tips of the bracts to form points.
8. Mark further lines down the outside of the bracts with the Dresden tool from the tip to the base. Roll the tip between the fingers until it resembles a witch's hat.
9. Paint the second calyx shape with Tylose glue and pull the wire through the centre securing it to the base cone.
10. Dust with yellow and then lime powder colour leaving the white area lightly shaded.
11. Overdust the top with lemon.
12. Spray with a 50/50 mixture of confectioners glaze and isopropyl alcohol.
13. Leave glaze to dry.
14. When dry dust the middle of the bud with a little flesh powder colour. This gives a natural powdery pollen look.
15. Tape with ¼ width mid-green florist tape.

Bougainvillea

These inconspicuous flowers are surrounded by papery boat-like bracts. The bracts are usually brightly coloured in shades of magenta and purplish pinks depending on the species, however, the white bougainvillea has its own simplistic beauty. The plant, which is native to South America, has been voted the world's most spectacular vine.

Materials

White flower paste

Powder colours: emerald, lemon, snow, viridian, lime, yellow

Confectioners glaze

Tylose glue

Isopropyl alcohol

Cornflour

33 & 30 gauge wire

Tiny blossom cutter – refer template

Bougainvillea cutter

Poinsettia petal veiner

Bougainvillea leaf or veiner

Light green florist tape

Modelling tools

Small cell stick and plastic toothpick

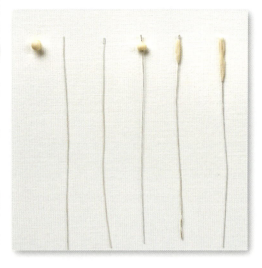

Flower (Centre)

1. Cut ⅓ length 33 gauge wire and hook the end tightly over by approximately 3mm.
2. Roll half a small pea-sized ball of white flower paste onto a hooked 33 gauge wire. When doing this make sure that the hooked end of wire stays at the top of the paste. Note: to make the tip very thin pinch off the top and re-flatten slightly.
3. Mark 3 grooves down the sides using the Dresden or veining tool.

Flower

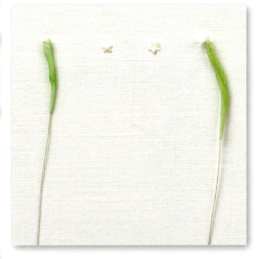

1. Roll out white flower paste very thinly until almost transparent and cut out 1 small blossom as per template.
2. Frill the edges with a plastic toothpick or the end of a small paintbrush.

3. Paint the top of the flower stem with Tylose glue and place the frilled flower shape on top of the stamen. Make a small indent with the sharp end of the small cell stick in the middle of the flower head. Press gently together with the cell stick in the centre and encourage the frills upwards.
4. Mix a little emerald with lemon powder colour and cornflour on a double white tissue. Blend the colour well and apply a little in the middle of the flower head and all the way down the sides using a soft flat-ended paintbrush.

Note
There are only 3 flower heads to each cluster of bracts. Not all the flowers have blooms on top; some just have the grooved flower stems which have a slightly rounded but flat finish. The top always remains white.

Bracts
There are 3 bracts to every 3 flowers.
1. Cut out 6 bracts in white flower paste which has been rolled extremely thin.
2. Cut ⅓ length 30 gauge wire.
3. Paint a strip of Tylose glue on 3 of the bracts from the top to the bottom.
4. Place the wire on top of the glue and then place a second petal shape over the first petal shape making sure that it matches exactly.
5. Using the small cell stick, gently thin the paste on either side of the wire, making sure not to roll over where the wire has been inserted (as this may cause the wire to protrude).
6. Recut the shape with the metal cutter.
7. Vein with the poinsettia petal veiner making sure that the centre wire is in the centre vein marking on the veiner.
8. Ball gently on a petal pad with the rounded edge of large cell stick or large balling tool to give movement.
9. Gently curve the petal backwards supporting it between the fingers while doing so.
10. Shape the side a little inwards towards the central vein.
11. Repeat twice more so you have 3 bracts in total.

Assembly and Shading
1. Using ¼ width mid-green florist tape join 1 flower and 1 bract together making sure that both bases meet and that the bottom 1cm of the flower fits snugly against the bract (in nature these are fused together).
2. Repeat with all 3 bracts and flowers.
3. Tape 3 bracts in a triangular shape one by one. Bend the stamens towards the centre after the bracts are taped together.
4. Shade the centre of each petal from the base a little way upwards using the emerald and lemon powder colour mix to give the flower depth.
5. Mix snow with a little cornflour and overdust the bracts. The snow gives the bract a realistic white velvety texture. Do not use snow by itself as it will not blend into the paste.

Leaves
1. Mix light green flower paste.
2. Roll paste out extremely thinly and cut out 2 leaf shapes.
3. Paint a strip of Tylose glue down the centre and place a ⅓ length 30 gauge wire down the middle by firmly pressing it down with the finger.
4. Place the second petal on top of the first.
5. Re-roll either side of the wire with the small cell stick to thin. Re-cut the shape with a leaf cutter.
6. Vein on a general purpose leaf veiner or on the back of a real leaf.
7. Ball the edges with a large balling tool to give slight movement.
8. Shade by dusting both sides of the leaf with yellow. Then gently dust with lime and finally a hint of viridian to give depth of colour to the leaf.
9. Spray with a 50/50 mixture of isopropyl alcohol and confectioners glaze and leave to dry.

Tip
It is much easier to spray the leaves with the glaze mixture as it is less messy than dipping and achieves a better result.

Anthirium

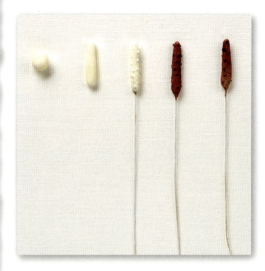

This flower belongs to the Arum lily family. There are between 600-800 different species of Anthirium which is also referred to as the Flamingo Flower or Boy Flower. The Mini Gem Anthirium is a complex cross-hybrid and is characterised by its tulip type Anthirium grace and elegance. The leaves can be spatulate, rounded or obtuse at the apex and can, in drier regions, have a nest-like look.

Materials

White flower paste

Powder colours: rubine, rose, brown, yellow, snow, lime, apricot, orange, gold, P pink

Tylose Glue

Confectioners glaze

26 gauge wire

Anthirium/Arum cutter

Anthirium veiner

Pin or metal satay stick skewer

Jem Hook tool

Modelling tools

Spadix

1. Roll a 5mm gauge size ball of white paste in the palm of the hand firmly to remove cracks (which weaken the paste structure).
2. Hook the end of a ⅓ length 26 gauge wire.
3. Roll the ball of paste into a sausage shape, measuring 20mm in length, which has a slightly round and pointed end.
4. Dip the end of the hooked wire into Tylose glue and insert into the full length of the sausage shape.
5. Secure the base of the sausage to the wire by firmly pinching the paste with the fingers.
6. Using a small metal satay skewer, prick the paste and indent flicks or peak shapes all over the sausage-shaped spadix.
7. Dust with rubine and a hint of brown and rose powder colour which has been blended on a double white tissue.
8. Spray with confectioners glaze and leave to dry.
9. When dry, dust the base with a little snow colour using the same pink dusting brush.

Spathe

1. Roll out white flower paste very thinly.
2. Cut out 1 petal shape.
3. Cut a groove with the tip of the cutter into the base of the spathe. Round off slightly using a pair of scissors.
4. Vein on the Anthirium veiner.
5. Dust with a 50/50 mixture of rose and rubine on both sides.
6. Ball the edges and pinch the top.
7. Turn the petal over and using the Jem hook tool slightly curve the outer edges inwards.
8. Using a large balling tool, ball the left and right bottom sides to give a slightly hollow look.
9. Re-vein if necessary.
10. Turn over to the right side of the petal.

Assembly of Flower

1. Moisten the base of the spadix with a little Tylose glue.
2. Insert the spadix wire into the spathe 2mm above the top of the cut groove base and secure.
3. The angle of the spadix to the spathe is 45°.
4. Secure the sides of the spathe to the spadix and then bend the top ⅓ backwards.
5. When dry spray with a 50/50 mixture of confectioners glaze and isopropyl alcohol.
6. Leave to dry. The flower is very waxy.
7. Tape the stem using white florist tape and then dust the stem with a mixture of brown and rubine.

Bud

1. Cut ⅓ length 26 gauge wire and hook the end tightly.
2. Moisten the hooked end with a little Tylose glue.
3. Roll a 5mm ball of white flower paste.
4. Insert the moistened wire into the paste ball and roll to form a rounded and slightly pointed top with a slightly larger rounded base.
5. Curve gently downwards.
6. Mark an indentation from the tip to the base on 1 side with a palette knife.
7. Shade with a mix of P pink and rubine and spray with confectioners glaze.
8. On very small buds or newly developing buds, the leaf unfurls exposing the pink bud. Therefore a leaf is semi-wrapped around the base of tiny buds.

Anthirium

Leaves

1. Colour a piece of flower paste light green and then roll it out on the grooved side of the petals board.
2. Cut out 1 leaf shape.
3. Cut ⅓ length 26 gauge wire and insert it into the leaf shape while the paste is still on the board. This makes the wire easier to insert as the finger is guiding it along the grooved area.
4. Vein using a general purpose leaf veiner or the back of a real Anthirium leaf.
5. Ball the edges to thin them slightly.
6. Dust with yellow and then overdust with a little orange down the middle and base area.
7. Dip into a 50/50 mix of confectioners glaze and isopropyl alcohol and leave to dry on bubble sponge, or hang upside down once the excess glaze has dripped off the paste leaf.
8. When almost dry, cup the bottom sides slightly towards the centre of the leaf.
9. Tape with mid-green florist tape.
10. Mix gold powder colour with a little lemon and isopropyl alcohol and paint in the veins using a toothpick or 000 pointed brush.

Tips

- The leaf must be completely dry before commencing to paint. If it is not, the gold veining will disappear into the green leaf and will not be visible.
- The beauty of this flower is its simplicity.

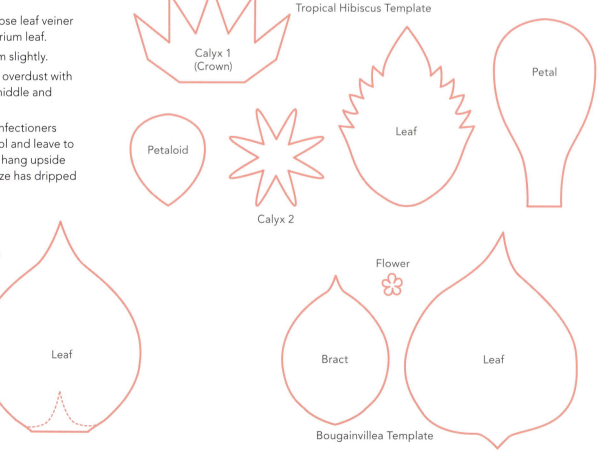

Tropical Hibiscus Template

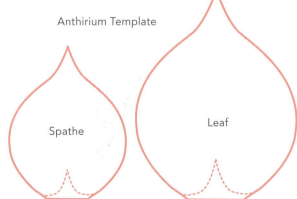

Anthirium Template

Bougainvillea Template

Exotic

Frangipani

Also known as the Lei flower, the frangipani is native to the tropical and subtropical Americas and Venezuela. They can grow up to 10 metres tall and the sweet-smelling flowers are widely used in tropical wedding arrangements. Colours range from white and apricot, to shades of pinks and even a deep red and burgundy.

Materials

White flower paste

Powder colours: yellow, lemon, orange, apricot, P pink, rose, rubine, pearl, brown, lime, viridian

28 & 26 gauge wire

Frangipani cutter

Large poppy veiner

Handy holder flower former

Jem hook tool

Cotton wool

Modelling tools

Petals

1. Roll out a small piece of flower paste very thinly.
2. Cut out 5 frangipani petals using a cutter or template.
3. Vein each petal using the large poppy veiner by placing each petal in the centre of the veiner and pressing down firmly. Note: Your paste should be superfine in thickness – so it is not necessary to ball the edges to thin them.
4. Place the petals on the petal pad. The petals should all have the bulging side on the right hand side.
5. Place the Jem hook tool horizontal and parallel to the top of the paste and 1 mm away from the inner edge on the paste side and skim the tool around the left edge of the paste until it reaches the bottom left hand corner. This will curl the paste upwards and inwards slightly and give a very realistic effect.
6. Repeat on the remaining 4 petals.

Flower Assembly

1. Take 1 petal and paint the base and 2mm up the stem with Tylose glue.
2. Place the second petal over the first petal ensuring that the left hand corners of the petals meet and the bases are at the same level. This creates a semi-fan formation.
3. Repeat the process with the remaining petals.
4. Paint a little Tylose glue on the left and right sides and in the middle a little way up the petal base only. Remove the excess glue with a finger – this will make things easier when attempting to roll the petals up to form the flower.
5. Dip fingers in cornflour (this prevents the paste from sticking to the finger) and roll up the flower tightly at the base, keeping the tops and base of the petals on the same level.
6. Roll the flower petals together in a tight formation from left to right or vice versa to form a slender stem.
7. Turn upside down and then gently roll out and thin the bottom 1cm to form a very slender stem measuring approximately 3cm in length.
8. Cup the fingers of your left hand (right hand if left-handed) to form a circle on top of the hand. Turn the flower upright and transfer into the left hand supporting the petals.
9. Gently and gradually open up the petals symmetrically.
10. Transfer to the handy holder drying rack to dry. Support with a little cotton wool if necessary until they are dry.

Tips

- When rolling the flower petals up, make sure that the first petal rolls over the last petal on the inner side otherwise the petal formation will be incorrect.
- There must be no visible hole through the centre of the flower as this will indicate that you have not rolled the flower correctly.
- Egg containers can be used to dry the flowers in. They can be dried upside down or cornflour can be placed in the egg container to support the flowers.

Wired Flowers

Wired flowers can be achieved by hooking the end of a 26 gauge wire and burning it into the end of a dried frangipani.

Alternatively, the tightly hooked wire end can be rolled into the flower.

Shading

1. Dust the centre with a mixture of yellow and lemon. Spread the yellow up each petal gradually using a soft flat ended dusting brush.
2. Dust the petals on both sides with P pink leaving some areas lighter than others.
3. For a darker pink shade, deepen the pink using a mixture of rubine, pearl and rose. Note: a little pearl colouring is all that is required. This gives a natural look to the petals.
4. Dust the middle outer edges with apricot.
5. Using a small pointed paintbrush, paint the centre with orange.
6. Blend all colours into one another well to prevent a blotchy look.

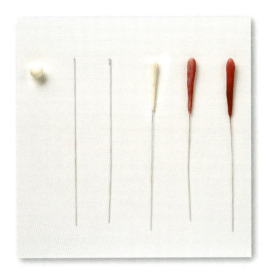  

Bud

1. Cut ½ length 26 gauge wire and hook the end.
2. Roll out a pea-sized ball of white flower paste firmly between the balls of the hands to remove any cracks (which would result in weakness in the finished product).
3. Moisten the hooked end of the wire with a little Tylose glue and insert into the ball of paste.
4. Roll the paste down the wire to form a teardrop (bud) shape, leaving the top ⅓ a little rounded.
5. Pinch the tip of the bud to form a point.
6. Mark indentations, extending from the tip to the base, into the bud with a sharp tool.
7. Slightly twist the bud on itself.
8. Dust with the same pink shading as per the flower but deepen the tones a little. The yellow shading is not required for the bud as these only apply to the open flower.

Leaf

As the leaves start to develop, they unfold from exactly half a leaf meaning there is only one side of the leaf from the central vein (this makes a great veiner if picked). As they mature, a full leaf develops, however, they are too large for use in sugar work on cakes, therefore developing leaves (scaled down in size) are used in this example.

1. Roll out a little light green flower paste on the grooved side of the rolling board. This works well as the central vein is very dominant.
2. Cut out 1 leaf shape using the template and insert ⅓ length 26 gauge wire.
3. If available use a real leaf as a veiner. Press the right side of the leaf against the wrong side of the real leaf using a small piece of sponge.
4. Gently thin the edges using a large balling tool on a petal pad or on the back of the hand.
5. Pinch the top tip inwards.
6. Dust all over with yellow and then overdust with a mixture of lime and brown mixed together. Deepen the tone slightly with a little viridian dusted at the base.
7. Mix a little isopropyl alcohol with a mixture of a little rubine and brown and paint the veined lines with a toothpick.
8. Steam to set the colour.
9. Spray the leaf with a 50/50 mixture of confectioners glaze and isopropyl alcohol.
10. Leave to dry slightly and then fold the leaf in half inwards and curve over the top third of the leaf.
11. Leave to dry completely and then tape with mid-green florist tape.

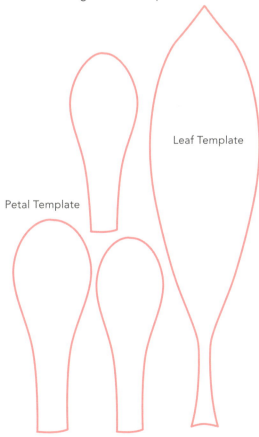

Leaf Template

Petal Template

Extension and Bridge Work

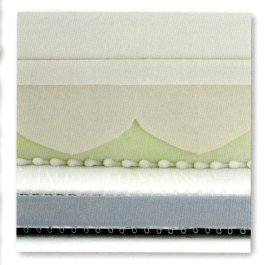

Bridge work is the term used when several even loops are piped directly onto the cake on top of one another, forming built-up lines which protrude from the cake. There are less time-consuming methods used by some decorators today, such as using modeled pieces of paste and attaching them to the cake, but the finished product does not have the same delicate impact as the traditional methods. Extension work compromises the vertical lines piped from the cake onto the bridge.

Materials

Royal icing mixed to medium peak consistency

Dried cake surface with piped snail trail base border

No. 0 & 1 writing tubes

Piping bags

Piping nozzle stand holder

Pin

Paper receipt/cash register roll

Scissors

Bridge Work

1. To ensure even spacing around the cake measure a length of paper receipt roll equal to the circumference.
2. Fold it in half lengthways.
3. Place one end on top of the other end and fold it in half several times until it measures approximately 2cm across ways.
4. Using a pair of sharp scissors cut a gentle curve from one side to the other, ending a little way up the other side of the paper.
5. Open out and wrap around the base of the cake securing the meeting points of the paper with a little sticky tape. Leave 3mm between the base border and the paper.
6. Pin-prick to mark the edges and the middle of each loop at the base and along the top.
7. Remove the paper.

8. Using a No. 1 writing tube and medium peak royal icing, pipe loops from dot to dot, piping over the marked dots. Ensure the first row of loops are attached directly to the side of the cake.
9. Pipe around the whole cake.
10. Repeat the previous step piping another 6 rows of loops directly on top of one another. Make sure that there are no gaps between the piped layers as this will cause weakness and possible breakage in the bridges.
11. Leave to dry completely, preferably overnight but at least a couple of hours. The stability of the dried royal icing creates the strength of the bridge to hold the design.
12. When the bridge is completely dry a thin film of soft peak royal icing can be painted on the inner side of the bridge using a fine paintbrush. This gives double strength and support to the bridge.

Note
There should be no gaps between loops.

Extension Work

1. Place a No. 0 writing tube in a piping bag and fill bag with a little medium peak royal icing.
2. Commencing at the upper marked dot, pipe a straight line downwards extending it at a 45° angle until almost touching the bridge. This stretches and straightens the icing which is pushed from the nozzle and sometimes has kinks in it.
3. Adjust the angle of the tube to go straight downwards and connect it to the bridge by letting the tube just touch the bridge.
4. Use a dry paintbrush to gently even out the meeting points of the bridge and extension.
5. The extension line must not sag in any way. Even pressure control in tube work is essential and will prevent this. The tube can be steadied with the aid of the other hand.
6. Should any breakages in piped lines occur, the broken lines must be completely removed with a hat-pin and not left lying in the bridge.
7. Pipe the next line close to the first line making sure that another line could not be piped between the first and second extension lines and that all lines are evenly spaced.

8. Continue piping in the same fashion around the entire cake. All lines must be piped at the same angle to one another (90°) unless a fancy pattern is planned.
9. Finish the extension work by piping a small snail trail on the top line of the extension work.
10. In this design small teardrops have been piped between the loop joins using a No. 0 writing tube.
11. Over-pipe the bridge edges with loops using the same No. 0 writing tube.

Suggestions
- Prior to piping the bridge, some shading can be done on the side of the cake where the extension work is to be piped. This gives a lovely finishing touch.
- A mirror image of the bridge can be marked and an alternative pattern created. The second bridge needs to be piped by turning the cake upside down.
- Ribbon can be inserted above the bridge.
- Flowers can be added to the joins of the loops or along the straight top edge.
- A patchwork look can be achieved by carefully piping across the extension at an angle.
- Embroidery or stenciling can be done above the extension work but this needs to be planned and done prior to commencing the extension work.

Troubleshooting
- Loops are sagging: The consistency of the icing is too soft or too much icing has been pushed too quickly out of the nozzle.
- Lines are breaking: Icing is too dry and crystals are causing weakness in the lines.
- Extension lines are not vertical: Loops have not been piped directly on top of one another at the joining points and are at a slight angle and therefore throw the whole pattern grid out of shape.
- Bridge breaks when piping extension lines: Too much tactile pressure is exerted on the bridge when lines connect. Weak areas have occurred due to gaps in the loops. Icing not totally dried.

Assembly

The two oval cakes are covered separately then secured on top of each other with royal icing. A snail trail border, delicate extension work and miniature frangipanis complete the detail on this versatile cake.

For a different look try replacing the bridge work with ribbon or experiment with different colours and your own creative ideas.

Flirty

Elegant and pretty in pink, this simple 3 tier round cake has a taller top tier so that the flowers cascade over the edge. A simple flowing spray, with some of the flower heads turned upwards, shows the fuchsias off to their best advantage. Delicate filigree butterflies add a whimsical dimension to the design.

Fuchsia

page 78

Filigree butterfly

page 81

Fuchsia

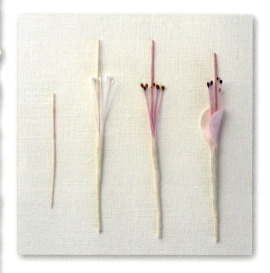

Stamens

The flowers have 7 or 9 stamens and a pistol. The anther tips are light brown or yellow in colour. The tip of the pistol is brown.

1. To make the pistol cut off the stamen heads and cover the stamen with paste. Work a small ball of paste up the stamen by rolling the paste on a board using your fingers.
2. Tape the pistol to a piece of 24 gauge wire and secure well.
3. The pistol is much longer than the length of the stamens, so add the stamens lower down on the wire.
4. Tape the stamens securely.
5. Dust the stamens a pale pink with dusting powder.

Fuchsia The fuchsia is indigenous to South America and New Zealand, however, the plants are found all over the world. There are more than 100 species and over 8,000 hybrids. The flowers are bell shaped and hang downwards. Sometimes they are described as earrings or ballerinas. Fuchsias range from white, pink, red and violet to several colour combinations and can be double or single. The calyx and corolla are often different colours.

Materials

White flower paste

Powder colours: rose, rubine, Barney, P pink, lime, yellow, viridian, brown

28, 26 & 24 gauge wire

Long fine white stamens

Fuchsia cutters or templates

White florist tape

Flower hanger

Modelling tools

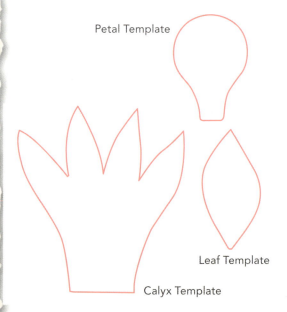

Petal Template

Leaf Template

Calyx Template

Flowers

The corolla of the fuchsia is usually quite one dimensional in colour, without too much shading. When iced, however, the flower tends to look quite lifeless without some shading, particularly if you are using the paler colours. Use some artistic judgement to colour the edge slightly to create depth.

1. Roll out a small piece of pale pink paste (the thinner you can roll out the paste for these flowers the better).
2. Cut out 4 petals and wrap them around a knitting needle or kebab stick to make them tube shaped.

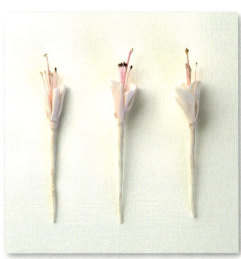

3. Using a little Tylose glue place the rolled petals around the bunch of stamens. Some petals curl around the stamens, others form as halves and sit next to the stamens.
4. Cut out 4 more petals and ball the edges, then wrap them around the first 4 evenly. Allow to dry slightly.
5. Roll out another 4 petals and ball a slight hollow into the middle of each petal.
6. Attach these 4 petals with the hollow to the outside.
7. The last layer of petals are small. Take a petal and cut it in half, then ball it out slightly.
8. The small half petals form the last layer and sit just inside the hollow of the previous row of petals.
9. Pinch the base of the flower to neaten and allow to dry until it is firm.
10. The group of petals form the corolla of the flower.

Calyx

The calyx has 4 sepals and some varieties have bright, vibrant colours. The sepals are quite long and curl up over the tip of the buds. As the buds burst and the flowers open, the calyx curls right back.

1. Roll out a piece of flower paste in the colour you have chosen.
2. Cut out the calyx.
3. Take the calyx and wrap it around the flower ensuring that the sepals are evenly spaced.
4. Work the long stem piece down the wire until it is secure and smooth. Work away the join with your fingers until it is invisible.

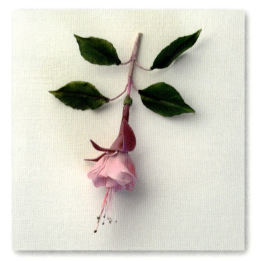

5. The base has a little green swelling, which later forms into the seed pod. Place a small ball of green paste at the base of the calyx stem to form a pod.

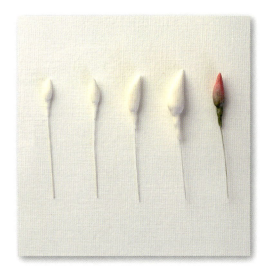

Bud

1. Take a small pea-sized ball of paste and form into a cone shape.
2. Hook a piece of 28 gauge wire and insert it into the base of the cone.
3. Pinch the base to secure and shape the base to form a bulge at the base of the bud.
4. Use a small ball of green paste where the bud ends to form the beginnings of the pod.
5. Make buds in various sizes. The smallest are greener in colour and the bigger buds are the same colour as the calyx.

Leaves

The leaf is similar to a rose, but the serrated edge is not as even or as pronounced as the rose.

1. Roll out a piece of paste, light lime green in colour.
2. Roll the paste on a grooving board to form a ridge in the middle.
3. Cut out a leaf with the cutter or template and insert a 28 gauge wire into the thickened part of the leaf, ¼ of the way up.
4. Smooth the edges with a balling tool and place onto a leaf former to create the veins of the leaf.
5. Take a cell stick and pull on the underside of the leaf to serrate the edges. By marking on the underside, the top of the leaf will not be harmed by the dragging of the tool.
6. Dust the leaf with lime and viridian dusting colours to create a realistic leaf colour. Dust the base with a little rubine.
7. Some varieties have pink veins. When the leaf has been dusted green, take a thin brush and, using rose, colour the central vein and some of the lateral veins. The base of the leaf is also pink on the underside.
8. The stems of the variety used were also pink in colour, creating an interesting contrast on the leaf.

Butterfly Template

Filigree Butterfly

Filigree Butterfly

1. Pipe each wing separately.
2. Using a No. 0 writing tube, pipe the outline of the first wing.
3. Pipe the connecting lines that separate the wings, and the more defining lines, with the No. 0 writing tube to give additional strength to the wing.
4. Using a No. 00 writing tube, pipe the finer trellis lines inside the wing.
5. Take care to end each strand of royal icing neatly and to connect all the lines to the main supporting outline of the wing.

The filigree butterfly adds a special touch to this elegant cake. The delicate detail requires a lot of practice and a steady hand but is quite easy to make.

Materials

No. 0 & 00 writing tubes
Royal icing medium peak consistency
Perspex or glass sheet
Acetate paper
Piece of bubble foam sponge
Fine paintbrush

Filigree Butterfly

6. Use a fine paintbrush to neaten edges.
7. Over-pipe the outline and main supporting lines with the No. 0 writing tube – this will neaten the design and add strength to the filigree butterfly.
8. Do the second wing in the same manner.
9. Allow the wings to dry completely, usually overnight.
10. Once dry, carefully remove from the cellophane paper.
11. Make a body on the cake by piping a few lines one on top of the other using a No. 0 writing tube to form a sausage shape.
12. Place the 2 wings into the centre of the piped lines and support them in an open position with a piece of foam.
13. Pipe a large dot to form a head. Insert 2 little stamens to form feelers.
14. Add the butterfly to an arrangement of flowers or fix to the side of a cake to add delicate interest.
15. The butterfly can be dusted with lustre dust to give it a shimmer or you can colour the wings with dusting colours.

Tips

- Filigree work is very intricate and delicate. It is done using a No. 00 writing tube, with a No. 0 writing tube used for over-piping the main skeleton of the butterfly piece.
- The design needs to be clear and secured firmly to a board with tape before beginning. The piping is then done on acetate or cellophane paper, which is nice and clear, as it releases the design easily when the piece is dry.
- The piping is done using medium peak icing and it is very important that the icing is well-made, lump free and of the correct consistency.

Lace Point Template

Assembly

Wire the flowers and leaves to form a spray, allowing the flowers to droop gently. Because of the nature of the shrub and its flowers they are difficult to arrange on a cake so this method works best.

A simple pink ribbon finishes off the base of each layer and a basic snail trail beading has been used to seal the cake. Lace points in the shape of a fuchsia complement the design and add a final delicate touch to the design.

Inspired

This 'inspirational' cake incorporates modern design elements with a spectacular display of wild flowers and foliage.

The unusual three-tiered formation creates an interesting juxtaposition between the cake and the floral elements, while the use of rich earthy tones gives the overall design a contemporary feel making it suitable for many different occasions.

Butterfly iris
page 86

Didgery sticks
page 89

Dietes flower
page 90

Jacaranda
page 94

Gum nuts
page 97

Butterfly Iris

Dietes Iridaceae Also known as the Japanese Iris and Moraea Iris, this flower is part of the *Dietes* family. The genus name is derived from the Greek words *di-* meaning two and *etes-* meaning affinities.

Materials

Flower paste

Powder colours: snow, Barney, turquoise, yellow, lemon, brown, flesh, emerald

Tylose glue

Cornflour

Isopropyl alcohol

33 & 24 gauge wire

Butterfly Iris cutters

Light green florist tape

Modelling tools

Centre Petals

1. Cut ⅓ length 33 gauge white wire.
2. Roll out white flower paste very thinly and cut out 2 of the smallest petals. Paint a strip of Tylose glue down 1 of the petals. Place wire over the glue making sure that the wire starts only ⅓ of the way down from the top of the petal tip. Place second petal on top of first petal.
3. Using the small cell stick stretch the paste outwards on either side of the central vein.
4. Use the sharp pointed end of the smallest cutter and cut a 'V' approximately 3mm long into the tip of the wired petal. Pinch each tip together and gently curve the petal inwards.
5. Dust with a 50/50 mixture of Barney and turquoise mixed with a little cornflour, leaving the base a little lighter. Repeat to make 3 petals in total. Bend each petal back 90° by holding the base where the wire meets the paste and supporting the paste between the fingers while bending the wire backwards. Tape together in a triangular formation using light green florist tape. Repeat to make 3 inner petals.

Butterfly Iris

Middle Petals (2nd Row)

1. Cut 33 gauge white wire in ⅓ length.
2. Using the second largest cutter and white flower paste cut out 2 petals.
3. Repeat wire insertion method as used in smaller petals and then stretch either side of the central wire and thin the flower paste. Re-cut with the same size cutter.
4. Stretch the top to form a slight point.
5. Vein using the upper left or right corner of the large poppy veiner.
6. Using the smallest balling tool, ball the inner top edges of the petal and then gently bend the petal forward.
7. Dust with a mixture of snow and cornflour mixed together. This gives a brighter white look.
8. Paint very fine stripes about 2mm long with a mixture of flesh and a hint of brown mixed with isopropyl alcohol from the bottom to ⅓ of the way up the petals.
9. Tape outside and in between each petal of the previous layer of petals with light green florist tape.

Outer petals

1. Cut out 3 petals using the largest shape cutter and insert ⅓ length 33 gauge white wire into each petal as per previous instructions.
2. Thin either side of the central vein and re-cut the petals with same size cutter.
3. Vein with large poppy veiner and bend slightly backwards from the bottom ⅓ and then slightly inwards on the top ½ of the petal.
4. Whiten the petals with snow and cornflour mix dusted on with a flat-ended paintbrush.
5. Dust the base and ⅓ of the way up the middle of the petal with lemon and yellow mixed 50/50. Overdust with yellow leaving a hazed look of the previous colour all around.
6. Repeat to make 3 petals.
7. Tape outside and in between second layer of petals.
8. Shade the centre of the flower with a hint of emerald mixed with cornflour.

Centre Petal Template   Middle Petal Template   Outer Petal Template

Inspired

Leaves

Leaves are very long and thin and measure around 1cm across horizontally. They can measure up to 30cm plus in length but are scaled down in proportion for use in cake decorating.

1. Use a full length 24 gauge wire.
2. With light green flower paste roll a sausage from halfway down the wire to the top of the wire by pulling the wire downwards while rolling up the wire.
3. Flatten the sausage shape on a rolling-out hard board with rolling pin. Re-cut into a conical shape if necessary.
4. Dust with yellow and then lime on a double white tissue using a flat-ended soft dusting brush.
5. Hold the wire between the fingers. Wrap a tissue around the wire only and spray with a 50/50 mixture of concentrated confectioners glaze and isopropyl alcohol.
6. Let the tissue absorb the excess dripping and then hang upside down on a drying rack to dry.
7. Tape to the bottom with light green florist tape.

Buds

1. Cut ⅓ length 24 gauge wire and hook the end tightly.
2. Roll out a 2cm diameter ball of white flower paste and form into a sausage shape approximately 4cm long and then slightly pinch both ends.
3. Mark 9 grooves down the bud using the flat end of the spatula and vein with large poppy veiner.
4. Mark 3 holes in top of the bud using the pointed end of a toothpick.
5. Take the small circle end of a ball-point pen (or piping tube) and indent a circle around the 3 marked holes at the top of the bud.
6. Dust with yellow and then overdust with lime and x green. Dust the circled area with a hint of brown mixed with cornflour making it a light sandy brown colour.

Stem, Bud and Flower Assembly

1. Thicken the base of the flower with a little lime flower paste tapering it down gradually.
2. Tape in a bud about 3cm from the base of the flower. The base of the bud should be taped tightly and closely to the flower stem.
3. Thicken the stem again with paste after taping in the bud, tapering it to a very narrow width at the bottom of the stem. This is not necessary for a spray formation but is necessary for a specimen flower.
4. Overdust with a little lemon and lime mixed together.

Didgery Sticks

Method

1. Cut a ½ length 24 gauge green wire.
2. Roll small amounts of flower paste ⅔ of the way up the wire with firm pressure by pulling down on the wire as you are rolling up the wire.
3. Roll flat using a rolling pin or large cell stick.
4. Trim on either side of the wire and re-roll on a balling mat to smooth.
5. Dust with lime all over and then with viridian ⅓ of the way down gradually lightening the shade going up the stick.
6. Dust horizontal stripes 1cm apart all the way up the stem. Finally dust the top 5cm with yellow powder colour.

Baloskion pallens These sticks are native to New South Wales and Queensland, Australia and are found in sandy coastal swamps with high water tables. They are clumps of leafless sticks growing up to 1 metre tall. They provide a modern accent to sugar floral art.

Materials

Pale green flower paste

Powder colours: lime, brown, lemon, viridian, orange

24 gauge green wire

Modelling tools

Dietes Flower

Dietes Bicolor Also known as African Iris or Fortnight Lily, this species is native to South Africa. Blooms are a light lemon to yellow with dark purple spots surrounded by an orange haze and grow in clumps.

Materials
White flower paste

Powder colours: lemon, brown, violet, yellow, orange, snow, white, lime, emerald

Tylose glue

33 & 28 gauge wire

Rose petal cutters

White and mid-green florist tape

Large poppy veiner

Corn veiner

Small scriber or cocktail stick

Large and small cell sticks

Modelling tools

Centre Petal
1. Cut a ⅓ length 33 gauge wire.
2. Roll flower paste out very thinly and cut out 2 of the smallest shaped rose petals.
3. Place both shapes side by side and using the large cell stick stretch to make them longer.

Dietes Flower

4. Paint a strip of Tylose glue down the middle of the petal and place 33 gauge wire on the top of the glue. Place the second petal on top of the first petal. Secure with forefinger down the central wire.
5. Place small cell stick parallel to the wire (but not over the wire) and thin both sides of the flower petal a little more.
6. Re-cut the petal with same cutter.
7. Using the rounded edge of the small cell stick ball the top edge firmly to create a little movement.

8. Using the pointed end of the rose cutter make a V shape in the middle of the rounded top of the petal.
9. Pinch the central vein together with angled tweezers from bottom to top.
10. Dust both sides with lemon. Repeat the process to make 3 small petals.
11. Bend the wires back at a 90° angle and tape together in a triangular formation using white florist tape.

Petals (2nd Layer)

1. Cut ⅓ length 33 gauge wire.
2. Roll out white flower paste thinly and cut out 2 of the second sized rose petal cutter shape. Paint a Tylose glue stripe down the centre of 1 of the petals and place the wire on the top of the glue then place the second petal on top of the first petal and secure.
3. Re-roll and thin petals on either side of the central vein using the small cell stick and re-cut with the same size cutter.
4. Stretch out the top ¼ to form a pointed petal and vein using the large poppy veiner.
5. Ball the edges to form very slight movement and frill the top ⅓ of the petal.
6. Pinch with angled tweezers to form a central ridge down the petal.
7. Shade with lemon and gently curve backwards.
8. Repeat process twice resulting in 3 petals.

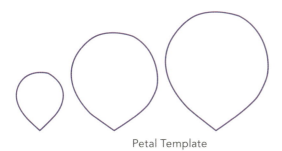

Petal Template

Inspired

Outer Petals

1. Repeat the process as for the previous 3 petals using the larger size cutter to make another 3 petals.
2. Shade all over with lemon and paint fine dots on the bottom ⅓ of the petal using a mixture of yellow and a hint of brown and orange mixed with isopropyl alcohol.
3. Blend a little violet powder colour with a hint of brown and isopropyl alochol. Using a fine brush paint a half circle shape above the painted dots approximately 5mm in diameter.
4. Finally shade the outer top edge of the circle with a light orange haze.

Buds

The bud can vary in size from between 5mm to 1.5cm in length. The top can also vary in size to between 5mm-1cm across.

1. Roll out a pea-sized ball of white flower paste firmly between the balls of the hands to remove any cracks (which will cause weakness in the paste).
2. Roll desired bud size down a hooked 28 gauge wire. Flatten the top.
3. Mark a tiny hole in the middle of the flattened top area and then mark down 5 indentations with a trowel from the top to the bottom of the bud.
4. Take a smaller circle than the top diameter measurement of the bud and indent into the paste slightly. Round off the sides gently.
5. Dust with a mixture of lime and yellow mixed 50/50 and then overdust with emerald.

Assembly of Flower and Bud

1. Bend back the petals at a right angle (90°) supporting the base of the petal between the thumb and forefinger when bending.
2. Tape the 3 smallest petals in a triangular shape.
3. Tape 3 of the next size petals in between and underneath the first layer of petals.
4. Tape the 3 largest petals in between and underneath the previous layer of petals. Adjust shape if necessary.

Flower and Bud

1. Over-tape from the base of the flower to the bottom of the stem with light green florist tape. Tape down 1cm and add a bud to 1 side.
2. Roll another ball of white paste and insert the wire into the paste from the bottom of the stem to the base of the bud.
3. Form a sausage shape, which has a fatter middle, and mould into a conical shape thicker in the middle and tapering at both ends. Mark a groove across from left to right, top to bottom, and dust in the same shading as the bud. This forms the swelling in the stem surrounding the base of the flower.

Leaves

The leaves are very long and thin.

1. Mix light green flower paste using emerald powder colour.
2. Cut a ½ length piece of 28 gauge wire.
3. Roll out a long piece of green paste and cut out 2 large conical shapes measuring approximately 2cm across and 15cm long.
4. Paint a stripe of Tylose glue down the middle and place the wire over the glue. Place second leaf shape on first and secure. Re-roll to thin paste and re-cut the original shape.
5. Vein using the corn veiner by pressing the paste onto a piece of dried corn leaf using a small section of sponge so that it does not stick to your fingers.
6. Fold the leaf in half and thin the edges with a large balling tool. The leaf is very linear and does not have much movement.
7. Shade with yellow on a double white tissue and then overdust with lime and then emerald.
8. Spray with a 50/50 mixture of isopropyl alcohol and concentrated confectioners glaze and leave to dry.

Tip

It is best to hold the wired leaf in a tissue and let the excess glaze drip off into the tissue and then hang it upside down to dry. The glaze prevents the leaves from absorbing moisture and also acts as a preservative.

Jacaranda

Centre

1. Cut 2 superfine stamens in half and tape 3 of them 1cm above the start of the tape to a 33 gauge white wire. Tape 1 stamen 2cm long onto the same wire with light green florist tape. This forms the pistol.
2. With a fine brush, paint the tips only with flesh powder colour mixed with isopropyl alcohol.

Bignoniaceae This species is native to tropical and subtropical South America and the Caribbean. It flowers in spring to early summer and each flower has a five lobed blue to purple corolla – sometimes white. The tree grows from two to 30 metres tall.

Materials

Flower paste

Powder colours: Barney, turquoise, violet, brown, flesh, snow

Cornflour

Isopropyl alcohol

33 gauge white wire

Superfine white stamens

Jacaranda cutter

Light green florist tape

Palm frond bark veiner

Bubble sponge

Modelling tools

Flower Template

Corolla

1. Cut out 1 jacaranda cutter shape.
2. Vein on palm frond bark veiner in a vertical direction.
3. Gently frill (flute) top edges with a small pencil size cell stick on a hard rolling board using a little cornflour on both the board and the paste to prevent sticking.
4. Paint a line of Tylose glue along the bottom of the petal shape and place the centre stamens and pistol on top of the glued line ensuring that the beginning of the taping is in alignment with the bottom of the paste. Paint a 5mm line of Tylose glue up both sides of the petal shape.
5. Roll the paste up from left to right tightly at the bottom. Turn upside down and roll between the fingers.
6. Place the large cell stick down the middle of the flower and press the 2 middle unjoined sides together, firmly pressing on the cell stick until the join disappears. It helps to have a little cornflour on the fingertips and cell stick when doing this to prevent sticking and breakage of the paste.
7. At this stage it may be advisable to change over to the small cell stick to get into the pointed end of the flower.
8. Indent ⅓ of the bottom area of the joined side with the forefinger as the jacaranda flower has a slightly squashed look in nature.
9. Lay on bubble sponge to dry or hang the flower upside down to dry.

Shading

1. Using a double white tissue and a flat-ended soft paintbrush mix 50/50 Barney and turquoise with a little cornflour to achieve a jacaranda purple colour. Add more cornflour until the right colour match is achieved.

2. Roll a pea-sized ball of cotton wool and place it down the throat of the flower on the side opposite the longer edged side of the flower.
3. Dust the flower with the jacaranda powder colour.
4. Remove the cotton wool and mix a little snow colour with cornflour. Paint the white area to make it brighter.
5. Dust the base with a little violet mixed with brown and cornflour for a deeper shade at the bottom of the flower.

Buds

The jacaranda buds are numerous and varied in size from very tiny to almost flower size.

1. Hook 33 gauge white wire ¼ length tightly. Paint with Tylose glue.
2. Roll a small ½ small pea-sized ball of white flower paste onto the hooked wire about 2.5cm in length.
3. Flatten the top and give it a slightly flat rounded look.
4. Using angled tweezers, pinch 5 lines in a circular formation to achieve a star-like look.
5. Indent the paste down the side of the wire with the Dresden or veining tool.
6. Dust with the same jacaranda purple mixture and then slightly over-dust with a hint of the deeper violet tone mixed with brown.

Note

Leaves are numerous and very small and not suitable for use in cake decorating as they are very time-consuming to make. One leaf consists of over 150 miniature teardrop shapes.

Gum Nuts

Method

1. Cut a length of 30 gauge wire into 6 and hook the ends tightly over to form a small, flat, looped shape.
2. Roll pinhead-sized balls of white flower paste.
3. Paint the hooked ends of the 30 guage wire with Tylose glue. Insert the balls of paste onto the wire.

Gum nuts create an unusual look in flower arranging and also add texture. The leaves of the gum nut tree have been omitted using artistic license.

Materials

White flower paste
Powder colours: flesh, brown
Isopropyl alcohol
30 gauge wire
24 gauge green wire
Fawn florist tape
Jem frilling tool
Modelling tools

4. Using the textured end of the Jem frilling tool mark a circle in the top of the ball and slightly flatten the top. Leave to dry fully. You will need to make around 20 balls per stem.
5. Paint with brown powder colour mixed with isopropyl alochol.

6. Cut a ½ length 24 gauge green wire. Twist a small pea-sized ball of paste down the top ⅓ of the wire in a sausage shape and then indent it all over with the top of the grooved Jem friller. Paint with the same brown colour.

7. Using a ¼ width fawn coloured florist tape start from the base of the paste and randomly tape the dried painted gum nuts in groups of 2-3 with intervals between them down the stem.
8. Re-paint over the entire sprig of gum nuts and taped stem with a mixture of brown and flesh.
9. Leave to dry.

Assembly

The spray has been wired together and attached to the three-tier cake using royal icing.

The base borders on the cakes have been piped with a No. 2 writing tube in a snail trail design.

The second tier of the cake has a 'floating' look to it – this is achieved by placing a smaller board between the two cakes. The top tier has been covered with sugarpaste on all sides and is secured to the second tier with royal icing to make it stand upright.

The cake board is covered and the sugarpaste impressed with the Jem fabric texture roller. A neutral russet colour ribbon is used to complement the spray rather than detract from the colours used.

Quirky

This is a modern cake with a free flowing arrangement of exotic spider orchids. The 'quirkiness' of the flowers is reflected in the unusual shape chosen for the cake.

The green leaves give form and shape, while the tree moss adds colour and interest. The cake is finished with an intricate lace pattern and would make a stunning statement piece for any celebration.

Spider orchid

page 102

Stamen extension

page 106

Tilansia (Tree moss)

page 108

Spider Orchid

Caladenia Orchids There are more than 70 species of these orchids which are endemic to Australia, New Zealand and New Caledonia. The plants have long spidery, perianth segments and range in colour from white, pink and red to yellow and lime green. The flowers can be quite large in size and because of the length of their slender twisted petals are quite fragile when made out of icing. You need to handle them with care as they break easily.

Materials

White and pale yellow-green flower paste

Powder colours: yellow, lime, lemon, emerald, x green, pearl, brown

Liquid colouring: medium-brown

Tylose glue

30, 28, 24 & 22 gauge wire

Template or cutters

Pale green florist tape

Modelling tools

Orchid Column

The column on this orchid is rather short and has a hooded look. Some have a little yellow anther cap on the tip.

1. Roll a small pea-sized piece of white flower paste.
2. Bend a hook at 1 end of a piece of 24 gauge wire.
3. Insert the hooked wire into the ball of paste.
4. Using a small balling tool, hollow out the ball of paste to form a fairly deep indent.
5. Roll an even smaller pea-sized piece of paste. Paint the hollow with a little Tylose glue, then press the pea-sized ball gently into the hollowed-out indent.

Spider Orchid

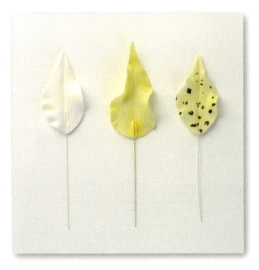

Labellum (Lip or Throat)

1. Roll out a piece of white flower paste using a grooved board, or roll the paste to create a thicker middle and thin sides. Cut out a throat using the template or a cutter.
2. Insert a 28 gauge wire into the thickened part of the petal.
3. Thin the edges on a petal pad using a balling tool. Lightly place onto a poppy veiner to create a few faint impressions.
4. Fold the petal in half and pinch a ridge from the tip to the bottom.
5. Pinch 2 little ridges at the base of the throat.
6. Twist the throat and curve the edges. Allow to dry on a piece of foam until it hardens.
7. Attach the column to the base of the petal and tape securely.

Dorsal Petal (Head)

1. Roll out white flower paste using a grooved board. Thin either side of the thick part until the paste is very thin.
2. Cut out the dorsal petal using a cutter or template.
3. Insert a 28 gauge wire into the thickened part. Vein using a grooving tool down the length of the petal.
4. Fold the petal in half down the centre to create a central vein.
5. Twist the narrow end of the petal and curl into a 'wonky' shape.
6. Allow to dry.

Lateral Petals (Arms)

1. Use the same method as above, curling and twisting the petals and bending the shape slightly backwards and the tips down.
2. The wider part of the petal is open with curved edges.
3. Allow to dry on bubble foam.

Labellum Template

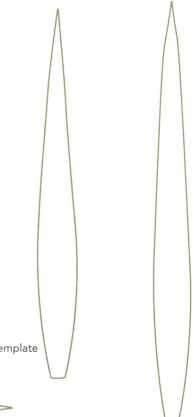

Dorsal Petal Template

Lateral Petal Template

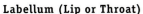

Leaf Template

103

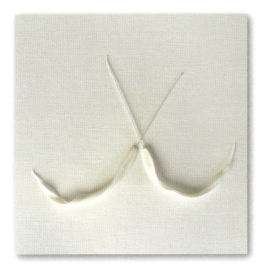  

Lower Lateral Petals (Legs)

The lower petals are the longest and most curved.

1. Cut 2 petals. Roll and form in the same way as the previous petals and allow to dry.

Colouring the Orchid

The column is lemon with a touch of green and has a few brown markings.

1. Colour the lip lemon and add a little pale lime mixed with lemon at the edges and base of the petal.
2. Paint uneven dots and splotches onto the throat of the petal in a light-brown colour using a toothpick or fine brush (dilute the liquid colour with water or alcohol if necessary).
3. Allow to dry, then steam to set the colour and give a sheen to the petal.
4. Dust all the other petals in the same manner. The outer petals are greener in colour than the throat, so use more lime and emerald mixed with cornflour to darken.
5. Colour the broader part of the petals with brown splotches and markings.

Assembly of the Flower

1. Tape the dorsal petal onto the column and lip.
2. Position the two lateral petals either side of the lip, forming two arms. Tape as neatly as possible and close to the base, where the wire meets the flower paste.
3. Lastly, position the 2 lower petals to form the legs, making sure the flower looks balanced.
4. Although the petals are long and twisted, they should be the same in length and shape.
5. Give the flower a quick overall steam taking care not to break the tips of the petals.

Buds

1. Roll a small ball of white flower paste into a thin, elongated teardrop shape. The tip is pointed and slightly bent.
2. Insert a hooked piece of 24 gauge wire into the thick end of the piece of paste.
3. Using a hat-pin, scratch a few lines along the length of the bud.
4. Make several buds, varying in size. The bigger the bud the larger the bulge and the longer it will be (approximately 5cm will be the longest).
5. The buds are taped up to form a stem, with the smallest at the top.
6. Dust the buds a medium green, blending a mix of emerald, lemon, lime and x green at the base of the bud.

Leaves

1. Use flower paste that is a pale green as a base colour for the leaves.
2. Roll out a long strip using a grooved board to form a thick centre down the length of the paste.
3. Cut out the leaf shape using a cutter or template or, alternatively, freehand.
4. Insert a 22 gauge wire that has been dipped in Tylose glue.
5. Place in a veiner, or use a grooving tool to create veins down the length of the leaf.
6. Fold the leaf down the centre to create a central vein.
7. Allow to dry. Dust with lime, and yellow. Dust x green down the centre vein. Steam to set the colour and spray with confectioners glaze mixture.

Assembly of the Arrangement

- The orchid plant has a bulb at the bottom, which we have not included, as it makes the arrangement heavy-looking. We have grouped the leaves together at the bottom. The orchid stems emerge from the centre of the leaves.
- This particular plant has a few thin, white aerial roots which emerge from the bulb. We have added a few for effect.
- Tape 1 or 2 of the flowers to the bud stem and arrange artistically.
- It is best to form a loose arrangement with these exotic flowers as they are large and the long petals tend to break.

Stamen Extension

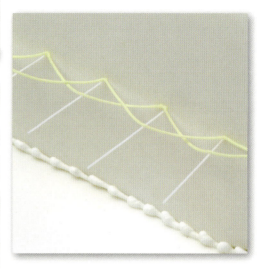

Stamen extension is very versatile. It is a technique that takes a bit of time to perfect but it is well worth the effort and gives a beautiful finish to the overall cake.

The stamens also provide additional strength and stability to the work.

Materials

One quantity of medium peak royal icing

Long fine stamens

No. 0 or 00 writing tube

Small paintbrush No. 0

Roll of receipt paper

Cellophane paper

Tape measure

Flat pin

Piping bags

Placing the Stamens

1. Wrap a piece of receipt roll around the circumference of the cake.
2. Allow the paper to meet exactly at the 2 ends.
3. Fold the piece of paper into equal sections. The number of folds will dictate how many stamens you will use and how close together they will be.
4. Make pencil marks on the paper where the folds are.
5. Wrap the paper around the cake and secure with a pin to hold in place. The folds in the paper will be evenly spaced, thereby ensuring that your stamens are placed equally around the cake.
6. Use the top edge of the paper as a guide when placing the stamens.
7. Insert the stamens where you have made the folds and the pencil marks. Make sure the heads of the stamens have been removed.
8. Cut each stamen the same length.
9. Push each stamen into the icing to the same depth. The stamens need to be perfectly spaced. Each one has to be the same length and they should all be level with each other.
10. Once the stamens have been placed, remove the paper.

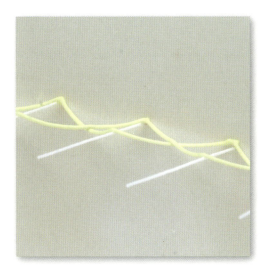  

Important

- Before you start doing the piping, check that your icing is of medium peak consistency. The icing should flow smoothly through the tube when continuous pressure is applied to the bag.
- If the icing is too soft the dropped lines will not hold and if it is too stiff it will be difficult to pipe with and will break easily.

Tips on Piping

- Place the cake at eye level with a good light source.
- If your icing hardens add a few drops of water little by little to soften the icing until you achieve the correct consistency.
- Keep leftover icing covered with a damp cloth at all times and cover with plastic wrap to prevent it from drying and forming lumps.
- Do not make too much icing.

Extension Work

The icing forms dropped strings, while the stamens form a permanent bridge.

1. Take a small amount of royal icing and mix in a little lemon powder colour.
2. Place a No. 0 writing tube inside a piping bag and ½ fill with lemon royal icing. Do not overfill the bag – ½ is more than enough.
3. Start piping from the side of the cake at the base of one of the stamens.
4. Keeping constant pressure on the bag bring the piped line away from the cake to ¼ way the up next stamen and back to the base of the following stamen, forming a V shape.
5. Repeat from the base of the next stamen.
6. Continue to repeat the pattern working the V shapes up to the tip of the stamens.
7. If the line breaks, remove the icing with a fine damp paintbrush.

Finishing Stamen Extension Work

- There are several ways of finishing off this type of work. The most common is to use piped dots or lace points.
- Here small lace points, in keeping with the shape of the spider orchids, have been used on the tips of each stamen.
- Small dots have been used in groups of 3 along the piped lines to form a picot design.
- The dots are purely decorative.
- A paste ribbon finishes off the cake where the stamens have been inserted.
- The cake is raised off the board creating the impression that the extension and cake are floating.

Tip

If your board is covered with sugarpaste, use cellophane to cover the sections of the board where you are working. Should lines break and drop this will prevent marks forming on the board.

Lace Point Template

Tilansia (Treemoss)

Tilansia Commonly known as Treemoss or Old Man's Beard. Part of the lichen family, these plants grow hanging from trees and resemble light grey/green hair. The lichen rely on moisture in the atmosphere in order to grow and are extremely sensitive to pollution. In the right moist conditions they sometimes grow up to several metres in length.

Materials

Light coloured grey/green flower paste

Tylose glue

28 gauge wire

Petal pad

Modelling tools

Method

1. Coat a piece of 28 gauge wire in the flower paste by rolling a small ball of paste along the length of the wire from side to side until it is coated very thinly.
2. Wind the piece of wire into a loose spring before the paste hardens.
3. Take very small pieces of paste and roll into thin slithers, pointed at each end, by rolling the paste on the petal pad with your fingers.
4. Dip one end of the slither of paste into Tylose glue and carefully attach to the wire.
5. Attach pieces along the length of the wire coil at different angles until you have a length of moss.
6. Attach to the cake with a little royal icing taking care not to put wire into the cake.

Tips

- Making the moss is very simple. The thinner you can make the little slivers the better.
- To make silver green flower paste mix a little silver powder colour with a hint of viridian.

Assembly

The flowers have been wired and placed into a posy pic, as a spray would be too heavy to be attached to the cake with royal icing only. The sprays are designed to flow over the edges of the board in keeping with the floating theme.

The asymmetrical cake is balanced by having a smaller arrangement in the front. The stamen extension work adds a different dimension and creates a delightful floating frill on the bottom of the cake. In competitive work, arrangements should not exceed the board size.

Romantic

From the charming champagne roses to the delicate purple liriope this lovely arrangement encapsulates romance.

An exquisite combination of flowers and techniques has been used to create this whimsical design, while the gentle colour tones and delicate finishing touches add an 'olde world' charm. This versatile bouquet can be used in a number of different settings.

Open champagne rose

page 112

Spider lily

page 118

Ixora

page 122

Royal purple liriope

page 124

Basket weave

page 126

String of pearls

page 128

Open Champagne Rose

Rosa 'Champagne' A shrub with dark-green leaves and clusters of pale champagne flowers. It blooms through summer and autumn. This rose epitomises sophisticated elegance and 'olde world' country charm. Its simplicity and neutral shading add a lovely dimension to this romantic design.

Materials

White flower paste
Powder colours: yellow, gold, brown, lemon, rubine, copper, viridian, lime, yellow, orange, brown, gold
Isopropyl alcohol & confectioners glaze
Tylose glue
Cornflour
Golden pollen (gelatine)
28, 24 & 22 gauge wire
Fine white stamens
Rose cutters
Mid-green florist tape
Large poppy veiner
Modelling tools
Bubble sponge
Grooved board

Centre stamens

1. Take a whole bunch of fine white stamens and fan them loosely to separate.
2. Mix yellow and gold together with a little isopropyl alcohol and colour the stamen heads and stems using a dusting brush.
3. Leave to dry.
4. Cut a ½ length of 24 gauge wire.
5. Leave 2cm of stamens exposed and then tape the stamens to the wire using ¼ width mid-green florist tape.
6. Taper the end of the stamens gradually by winding the florist tape around itself many times to prevent a bulge where the stamens join the wire.
7. Over-tape using full width tape.
8. Make a little rose pollen by mixing fine grade gelatine with yellow, orange, brown and gold powder colour and shaking it up together in a small sealed container.

Open Champagne Rose

9. Paint stamen heads with a little Tylose glue.
10. Dip the moistened stamen heads in the pollen.

Petals (1st Row)

1. Roll out a little white flower paste very thinly and cut out 3 petals using the first size petal cutters as per template.
2. Vein each petal on either top corner of the large poppy veiner.
3. Place petals on a balling mat and use the rounded end of the large cell stick to ball the edges to thin them and give slight movement to the petals.
4. Apply a little Tylose glue to the base.
5. Place the first petal 5mm above the stamen heads and wrap the moistened base around the wire.
6. Work from left to right and wrap the second petal halfway across the first petal in the same manner. Do the same with the third petal making sure the right hand side of the petal goes underneath the first petal.

Petals (2nd Row)

1. Cut out 3 petals using the same size cutter. Ball and vein them in the same manner as the first row.
2. Ball the centres using the rounded edge of a large cell stick.
3. Place a little Tylose glue on the bottom ⅓ of each petal.
4. Hold the flower stem upside down and, starting between any join in the first row of petals, attach the petals in the same manner as the first row. Space the petals evenly making sure that the centre of the petals is placed over the join.
5. Hang upside down to dry.

Petal Template

Romantic   113

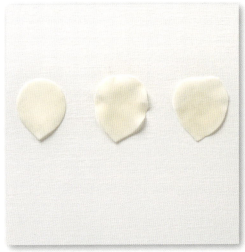  

Petals (3rd Row)

1. Using the next size cutter, cut out 5 petals and repeat the same method as previous rows.
2. Keep the spacing regular and even and place the petals in between the joins of the previous petals in the second row.

Petals (4th Row)

1. Roll out a small piece of white flower paste on a grooved board using the 2nd size groove.
2. Cut out 5 grooved petals. Keep them from drying out by placing them under a zip lock bag which contains a damp cloth.
3. Cut 5 x ⅓ lengths of 28 gauge wire.
4. Place each petal in the groove individually and then place the forefinger on top of the paste petal and feed the wire 1cm into the paste using the groove as a guide to ensure the wire is inserted straight. It is a good idea to dip the finger into cornflour to prevent it sticking when feeding the wire into the paste.
5. With a small cell stick, stretch the top ⅓ of the paste diagonally. This gives a very realistic look to the finished rose petals.
6. Vein on either top ⅓ of the large poppy veiner.
7. Place on the balling pad and gently ball the petal edges using the rounded edge of the large cell stick to give a slightly frilled look.
8. Turn the petals over and use a large glass balling tool to hollow the middle slightly and flatten the groove where the wire is inserted.
9. Place the hollowed side upside down on bubble sponge to dry.
10. Bend the wire at a right angle to the petal. The hollowed side is the underside of the petal.
11. Tape evenly around the previous layer, starting with the first petal in between any of the joins in the previous layer of petals and working from left to right. Tape each petal halfway across the previous petal and ensure the last petal is under the first petal.
12. Some flowers may require another petal in this row depending on the individual shape so it is wise to have a spare petal ready.

Petals (5th Row)

1. Repeat as per previous row only this time cut out 7 petals.
2. Tape the 7 petals around the 4th layer in the same way.
3. Leave the entire rose to dry completely.

Shading

1. Use a paintbrush to blend a mixture of lemon with a hint of yellow and a dash of gold on a double white tissue.
2. Using a flat ended dusting brush, dust the centre of the flower well and then lightly shade the outer petals for a realistic finish.
3. Dust the underside of each petal as well.

  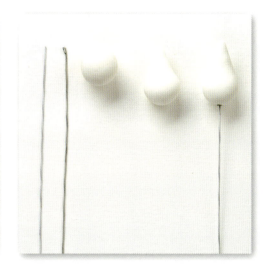

Calyx

On a closed rose or bud the calyx protects the bud and the enclosed petals.

1. Make a little light green flower paste.
2. Make a witch's hat by taking a small ball of green paste and pinching it in the middle to form a teardrop shape. Flatten the bottom of the teardrop with the fingers and then place it on a board. Roll the flattened area very thinly using the end of a paintbrush dipped in a little cornflour to prevent sticking.

3. Place the calyx cutter over the witch's hat and cut out one calyx shape.
4. Place the calyx on a balling pad and then stretch each sepal lengthways using a balling tool.
5. Mark a central vein down the individual bracts using the Dresden or veining tool.
6. With very fine embroidery scissors, make a 1mm x 4mm cut into either side of each bract.
7. Turn the calyx over and ball the middle with the rounded end of the large cell stick.
8. Paint the middle balled area and 2mm up each bract with a little Tylose glue. Be sure to remove any excess glue.
9. Take the dried rose and feed the stem through the middle of the calyx and up the stem till it reaches the rose petals. Secure gently and let the calyx bracts fall down as it is an open rose.

Bud

1. Cut ½ length 22 gauge wire.
2. Roll a 20mm diameter ball of white flower paste.
3. Place in the ball of the hand or on a balling mat and roll the top half to form a narrow cone shape.
4. Hook the end of the 22 gauge wire and then heat in a candle flame until it is white-hot.
5. Insert the white-hot wire very quickly into the bottom end of the cone until it reaches ¾ of the of the way up. This crystallises the sugar around the wire and secures the cone immediately, rather than having to wait for the glue to dry.
6. Neaten the base and leave to dry completely.

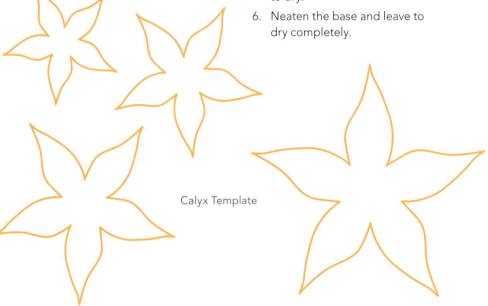

Calyx Template

Open Champagne Rose

7. Roll out 1 rose petal (size as per template) and thin the edges. Do not frill.
8. Paint a little Tylose glue ⅔ of the way up the petal and then place the cone ½ way up the petal and wrap around the cone ensuring that the top is not visible.
9. Repeat the same process with a second petal but this time place the cone in the middle of the join of the previous petal. When the petal is secure and wrapped, cup it outwards a little.

10. For the third row cut out 3 petals the same size and use the small cell stick to stretch them diagonally at the top of both sides. This gives a very realistic look to the rose petals.
11. Vein them on the top right or left corner of the large poppy veiner.
12. Place the veined petals on a balling pad and ball the centres with a large glass balling tool.
13. Turn the petals over and place them on a piece of bubble sponge to keep their shape.
14. Paint each petal with a little Tylose glue halfway up the petal.
15. Pick the petal up with the middle finger (the glue will stick it to the finger); turn the hand over and place the petal half way across the last join of the previous row. Work from left to right sticking the right side down and leaving the left unattached.
16. Place the second petal halfway across the previous petal and the third petal halfway across the second petal and then the right side of the petal under the first petal.
17. Shape a little and leave to dry.
18. Shade the same as the rose making the bud a little more intense in colour.

Calyx on Bud

The calyx on the bud is the same as on the rose but the bracts are closed around the bud. The bracts therefore need to be secured to the bud with Tylose glue which has been painted ¾ of the way up the bract.

Open Champagne Rose

Leaves

The rose leaf assembly consists of 1 large leaf at the top, 2 medium leaves and then 2 small leaves growing on 1 leaf stem.

1. Cut 5 x 28 gauge wires ⅓ in length.
2. Colour a little light green flower paste. The colour is important to the final shade of the leaf and must not be too dark.
3. Roll out on the smallest grooved side of the board.
4. Using the same technique as for the rose petals, insert the wire halfway up the leaf.
5. Vein the leaf against the back of a real rose leaf by placing the right side of the leaf on the wrong side of the real leaf and matching the central veins. Press down firmly on the leaf with a small piece of sponge.
6. Gently peel the paste leaf off the back of the real leaf being careful not to let the wire break through the paste.
7. Make 2 small, 2 medium and 1 large leaf for 1 spray of leaves.
8. Place on a balling mat and ball the edges gently to create movement.
9. Mix viridian with a little brown powder colour on a white tissue and blend it with a flat-ended dusting brush.
10. Dust each leaf all over.
11. Overdust the base with viridian.
12. Dust the top side of the leaf with a little yellow.
13. The leaf on the champagne rose is very dark. Different rose bushes have different coloured leaves so be sure to check the shade for each individual rose.
14. Steam over boiling water to set the colour by waving the leaf through the steam quickly and not allowing the leaf shape to change or soften too much.
15. Lay on a piece of bubble sponge and spray with a 50/50 mixture of confectioners glaze and isopropyl alcohol.
16. Leave to dry completely. Do not touch while drying as it will lift the colour off the leaf.
17. Tape with mid-green florist tape.

Assembly of Leaf

1. Cut ⅓ length 28 gauge wire and tape it with mid-green florist tape.
2. Gently curve it by stroking between the thumb and forefinger.
3. Tape halfway down each leaf stem with the same coloured tape.
4. Curve the leaf wires in the same fashion to create movement.
5. Tape the largest leaf at the top.
6. Leave 2cm and then tape in 1 medium leaf to the left and 1 to the right.
7. It is imperative to obtain a fine balance when taping by ensuring there is not too much space nor too little space left between the leaves.
8. Do the same with the smallest leaves.
9. If necessary curve slightly again for movement.

Leaf Template

Romantic

Spider Lily

Hymenocallis Littoralis The Spider Lily belongs to the family *Amarylidaceae*. There are 63 species which are native to sub-tropical America. It is also referred to as the Beach Spider Lily. The corona is like a beautiful membrane and the stamens and the tepals are partially fused to the corona. The large flowers are white with a light lime green centre and have the scent of vanilla.

Materials

White flower paste

Powder colours: emerald, lemon, snow, brown, pearl, violet, orange, yellow, brown, viridian, lime

Cornflour

Tylose glue

Confectioners glaze

Isopropyl alcohol

33, 28 & 26 gauge wire

Modelling tools

Spider lily pollen

Circle cutter as per template

Fine gelatine & small container

Mid-green florist tape

Palm frond section to vein

Stamens

1. Cut 6 x ½ length 33 gauge white wire.
2. Roll out a small pea-sized ball of white flower paste firmly between the palms of the hands to remove any cracks.
3. Insert the wire through the ball of paste and push it 8.5cm down the wire.
4. Squeeze the base of the ball to secure the wire and then roll the paste between the thumb and the forefinger in an upwards direction while pulling down on the wire with the one hand. This helps to make the wire as thin as possible and prevents the wire from bending.
5. Place the covered wire on the rolling board and, with the large cell stick, flatten the paste to make it thin.

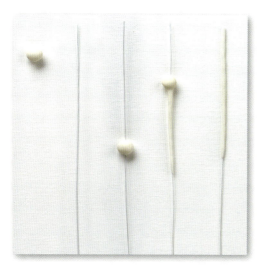

6. Use sharp scissors and cut away the excess paste on either side of the wire.
7. Place the wire on a balling mat and rub it backwards and forwards firmly with 3 fingers to even the paste.
8. Curve gently between the thumb and forefinger.
9. Make another 5. There are 6 stamens in total.
10. Blend a mixture of lemon powder colour with a hint of emerald on a double white tissue with a flat-ended paintbrush.

11. Place the stamen on a clean tissue and dust the stamen ⅔ of the way down from the top only. Leave the bottom ⅓ white. Dust all 6 stamens.

Anthers

The anthers are particularly narrow in the spider lily and measure approximately 1mm in thickness and 7mm in length.

1. Take half a glass pinhead-sized ball of flower paste and roll it firmly into a tiny sausage as per measurements above.
2. Paint the tip of the stamen with a little Tylose glue and secure the anther to the stamen by placing the centre of the anther on the glued stamen.
3. Leave to dry thoroughly.
4. Take a small amount of fine grade gelatine (semolina can be used as an alternative) and mix it with orange, yellow and brown powder colour to make pollen.
5. Paint the anther with a little Tylose glue and then wipe the glue away again so that the anther is only just moistened.
6. Dip the moistened anther into the pollen mixture ensuring that the entire anther is covered.

Note

If excess glue is used, too much pollen will adhere to the anther and it will look unnatural.

Pistol

There is one pistol which is 2cm longer than the stamens.

1. Repeat the stages for making the stamen but make the pistol 2cm longer and leave off the anther.
2. Dust the pistol with the same green as used to shade the stamens but dust it all the way down.

3. Roll a minute ball of white flower paste which is only just larger than the pistol width.
4. Secure to the top of the pistol with a little Tylose glue.
5. When dry, paint with a little brown and violet powder colour mixed together with a little isopropyl alcohol.
6. Leave the pistol straight. Do not curve.

Staminal Corona

This corona is a cup-like shape attached to the back of the stamens.

1. Roll a large pea-sized ball of white flower paste and squeeze the middle to form a teardrop shape.
2. Flatten the bottom with the fingers to form a witch's hat or Mexican hat shape.
3. Place on a hard rolling board and thin the flattened part using the small cell stick.
4. Pick it up and hollow using the textured end of the large cell stick dipped in a little cornflour to prevent sticking to the paste.
5. When hollowed, flute the edges by exerting gentle pressure on the paste using the large cell stick.
6. Paint the base of the pistol with a little Tylose glue.
7. Insert the pistol through the centre of the hollowed corona and gently squeeze to secure the paste to the wire.

Assembly of Staminal Corona

1. Cut mid-green florist tape into ¼ widths.
2. Place each stamen with the curve facing inwards. Bend each wire backwards at a 45° angle to the stamen and tape the six stamens individually around the corona with even spacing.
3. Tape to the bottom.
4. Paint a little Tylose glue on the bottom third inside area of each stamen and secure to the corona by pressing the corona against the stamen.
5. Dust the centre of the staminal corona with a little lemon powder colour mixed with a hint of emerald and a little cornflour.

Tepals

There are 6 tepals.

1. Cut a ½ length piece of white 28 gauge wire.
2. Roll a pea-sized ball of white flower paste 8cm down from the top of the wire.
3. Squeeze the base to secure.
4. Using the same method as the stamens, roll the paste up the wire to form a long narrow sausage.
5. Place the sausage shape on a balling mat and flatten with the fingers and then with a small rolling pin.
6. Using the small cell stick, stretch the paste on either side of the central wire in an outwards direction. Do not roll over the wire as this will cause the wire to penetrate the paste and be visible.
7. Use sharp embroidery scissors and cut a narrow convex shape from the stretched shape, measuring 5mm across the middle of the convex tepal. The ends must be pointed.
8. Vein each tepal with the textured side of the large cell stick (a piece of corn husk is also suitable).
9. Dust each tepal with a mixture of snow and cornflour with a hint of pearl powder colour.

Corona Template

Leaf Template

10. Pinch the tip of the tepal and then curve backwards gently by working the tepal between the thumb and forefinger to create natural movement.
11. Gently curve back both outer side edges of the tepal (this is barely noticeable).

Assembly of the Tepals

1. Using ¼ width mid-green florist tape, tape each tepal to the back of each stamen. The middle of the tepal is in the middle of the stamens.
2. Tape neatly to the bottom so the flower looks like a spider. Over-tape with full-width mid-green florist tape to thicken the stem.

Leaves

1. Cut ⅔ length of 26 gauge wire.
2. Colour a 3cm diameter ball of paste light green by using a little lime powder colour.
3. Roll out the green paste very thinly and cut out 2 large conical shapes as per template.
4. Place a strip of Tylose glue down the entire length of the paste.
5. Place the wire on top of the paste.
6. Place the second conical shape over the first shape and run the finger down the wire to secure.
7. Using the large cell stick, thin the paste on either side of the central wire. Do not roll over the wire.
8. Recut the original shape.
9. Place the leaf shape on a balling mat and ball the edges very lightly to create movement.
10. Vein against a section of palm frond by placing the right side of the wired leaf against the wrong side of the palm frond. Place a piece of sponge over the paste and press down firmly. The sponge will prevent the leaf from sticking to the fingers and will give a uniform vein to the leaf.
11. Remove the sponge and then re-ball the edges.
12. Place on a double white tissue and dust with yellow then viridian powder colour and overdust with lime.
13. Steam to set the colour.
14. Lay the leaf on a large piece of sponge, then glaze by spraying with a 50/50 mixture of isopropyl alcohol and confectioners glaze.
15. Leave to dry.
16. Tape the stem with mid-green florist tape.

Bud

1. Cut a ½ length piece of 26 gauge wire.
2. Roll a 1cm diameter ball of white flower paste 8cm down the wire.
3. Pinch to secure at the base and work it up the wire.
4. Pinch the top.
5. Mark 3 grooves vertically down the length of the bud.
6. Dust with a lemon powder colour, then a mixture of emerald and lemon. Finally dust the tip with a light lime green and blend the darker shading down the bud a little for a realistic look.

Tip

When balling the edges of anything, always place the balling tool half off and half on the paste and exert even pressure while balling. Never hold the end of the wire or paste whilst balling as this will cause your paste to tear.

Ixora

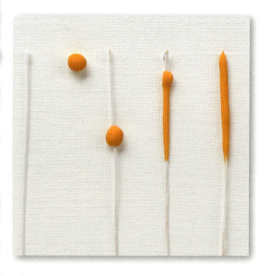

Genus Rubiaceae Ixora is also known as West Indian Jasmine and Jungle Flame and is native to tropical Asia. The flowers grow in brightly coloured cluster formations and are used in Hindu worship and Indian folk medicine. Colours range from vivid reds to orange tones and buttercup yellows. The leaves, measuring from 7-15 cm long, are leathery and grow in clusters at the base of the flower. The brightly coloured flowers have good impact and are a nice addition to a flower spray.

Materials

Light burnt orange flower paste

Powder colours: rubine, orange, apricot, lemon, snow, x red

Tylose glue

33, 28 & 24 gauge wire

Ixora flower & leaf cutters

Brown and mid-green florist tape

Double white tissue

Bubble sponge

Modelling tools

Flower

You will need to make many buds and flowers to form one cluster flower head.

1. Cut ¼ length 33 gauge wire and hook the end tightly.
2. Roll a pinhead-sized ball of orange flower paste 2cm down the wire and pinch the tip to form a point.
3. Take a small amount of the same coloured flower paste and roll out thinly. Cut out 1 petal using the cutter or template provided.
4. Ball the edges with a small balling tool.
5. Mark a hole in the centre with the sharp end of the small cell stick.
6. Paint a little Tylose glue on the top of the sausage shape.

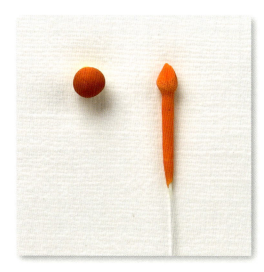

7. Insert the wire through the petal shape and secure leaving 1mm of the paste covered wire tip protruding from the petal.
8. Support the petal between the thumb and the forefinger and slightly flatten to curve downwards.
9. Tape the wire with ¼ width brown florist tape.
10. When the flowers are dry shade the centres using a fine brush and dust with a mixture of a little apricot and a hint of rubine which has been mixed together on a white tissue.

Bud

1. Cut and hook a ¼ length 33 gauge wire.
2. Take a double size glass pinhead ball of orange flower paste and insert it 2.5cm down the hooked wire.
3. Roll the paste up the wire exerting firm pressure on the paste until it reaches the top.
4. Form a rounded head on the bud by gently squeezing the paste over the end of the wire and then pinching the tip.
5. Mark 3 lines on the bud using the Dresden tool.
6. Dust the bud with a mixture of lemon powder colour mixed with a little snow.
7. Blend a little x red with isopropyl alcohol and then paint fine lines down the grooves of the bud using a toothpick.

Leaves

Leaves vary in size and can range from 7-15cm in nature. Smaller, more proportionate leaves have been used for this cake.

1. Cut a ⅓ length 28 gauge wire.
2. Roll out a piece of light green flower paste thinly and cut 2 leaf shapes using a leaf cutter or the template provided.
3. Place a strip of Tylose glue ⅔ of the length down 1 of the petals and then place the wire on top of the glue.
4. Place the second leaf shape on top of the first leaf shape and thin the paste on either side of the central wire. Re-cut the same shape.
5. Vein against the back of a real leaf by pressing the right side of the flower paste leaf against the wrong side of the real leaf. Make sure that the central veins lie on top of one another. Press down firmly using a piece of sponge. A general purpose silicone leaf veiner can also be used.
6. Thin the edges on a balling mat using a large balling tool to create movement.
7. Dust the central vein area with yellow and then dust the entire leaf with lime mixed with a hint of brown on a double white tissue and applied with a soft flat ended dusting paintbrush.
8. Pinch the tip and fold the leaf slightly inwards.
9. Bend the top ⅓ slightly backwards.

10. Steam to set the colour (by boiling a small amount of water and waving the leaf over the steam). The colour may deepen a little.
11. Lay the leaf on a piece of bubble sponge to dry. Make sure that the leaf has maintained its shape.
12. Spray with a 50/50 mixture of isopropyl alcohol and confectioners glaze.

Assembly of the Flower Cluster

1. Tape each flower and bud with a ¼ width brown florist tape.
2. Tape in a ⅓ length 24 gauge wire halfway down the first flower for strength.
3. Tape in flowers one by one in a cluster formation using mid-green florist tape. Tape the buds randomly about 1cm above the flowers.
4. There is no set amount of flowers or buds to any cluster. Groups of flowers can range from 7 to 25 or more.

Leaf Assembly

- The leaves grow inwards and directly off the thick stem.
- Tape each leaf from the base of the leaf directly onto the stem.
- There are no set clusters of leaves to one flower stem.

Ixora Leaf and Flower Templates

Royal Purple Liriope

***Liriope Muscari** Common name Lily Turf. This is a member of the lily family. It grows 60cm tall and 45cm wide and has strappy green leaves and bell-shaped purple flowers. It is incredibly hardy and makes a spectacular display when grown en masse. With its understated flowers and foliage it adds an elegant touch to any cake decoration – whether it is displayed as a specimen or incorporated in a spray formation.*

Materials

White flower paste

Powder colours: silver, Barney, snow, lemon, flesh, viridian, lime, brown, peach

Isopropyl alcohol

Tylose glue

33 & 28 gauge wire

Fine white stamens

Miniature 5 petal pointed daisy cutter

Fawn florist tape

Modelling tools

Sharp scissors

Balling mat

Large cell stick

Flowers

1. Take a whole bunch of stamens and paint the tips with a little lemon dusting powder mixed with isopropyl alcohol.
2. Roll white flower paste out very thinly and cut out a daisy using the cutter specified.
3. Place cut out shape on a balling mat and ball the centre to cup slightly.
4. Paint the base of 1 stamen with a little Tylose glue and feed the bottom of the stamen through the centre of the daisy being very careful not to tear the paste.
5. Gently secure daisy to the base of the stamen head with thumb and forefinger.
6. Leave to dry.

Note

Make approximately 30.

Buds

1. Cut a piece of 33 gauge wire into ⅕ lengths and hook the ends tightly.
2. Roll pinhead-sized balls of white flower paste and feed through the top of the hooked wire. Roll the paste 1mm down the wire to form a tiny teardrop shape.
3. Make varying sizes which are a pinhead and smaller.
4. Make approximately 3 times the number of buds per flower.
5. Cut ½ length 28 gauge wire and tape with fawn florist tape.
6. Mix 70% silver and 30% Barney on a double white tissue. Add a little snow powder colour and blend thoroughly with a paintbrush.
7. Dust all flowers and buds.
8. Thoroughly mix a little isopropyl alcohol with equal quantities of flesh and peach powder colour.
9. Paint the flower and bud stems with a fine paintbrush.

Assembly

1. Cut ¼ width fawn florist tape.
2. Start taping the spray of liriope with the smallest buds at the top. Tape in 4 buds fairly close together.
3. Tape the next bud 1cm down.
4. Tape another bud almost next to the fifth bud.
5. Randomly tape buds and flowers down the stem.

Leaves

1. Colour some olive green flower paste using viridian and a hint of brown.
2. Cut ⅔ of a length of 28 gauge wire.
3. Insert a pea-sized ball of green paste ⅔ of the way down the stem and squeeze gently to secure the paste to the stem.
4. Hold the wire with 1 hand and use the opposite hand to roll the paste up the wire by pulling the wire down at the same time as rolling the long sausage shape of paste up the wire.
5. Place the wired shape on the balling mat and firmly rub back and forth on the pad to even the paste.
6. Flatten and then roll over it lengthways using a large cell stick.
7. Pick the flattened leaf shape up and cut a long thin conical shape measuring approximately 8-10mm wide with 2 pointed tapering ends using fine embroidery scissors.
8. Use a large balling tool to thin the edges on a balling mat. Do not curl the leaf.
9. Dust with viridian powder colour and a hint of brown. Re-dust with viridian to build the colour and give depth, then overdust with a little lime.
10. Gently curve backwards.
11. Steam to set the colour and leave to dry.
12. When dry, spray with 50/50 confectioners glaze and isopropyl alcohol mix and hang upside down to dry.

Tip

When dusting delicate flowers, hold the flower head very closely, resting on the fingers, and then dust. This way there is no friction on the petal when dusting and less likelihood of breakage.

Liriope Template

Basket Weave

A woven basket is ideal for displaying flower arrangements like this country-style bouquet. Although the technique requires a little practice, the end result is well worth the effort.

Materials

Stiff peak royal icing
(refer royal icing section)

Powder Colours: gold, yellow, brown

Covered cake

Basket weave tube

No. 2 or 3 writing tube

Method

Basket weave can be executed using a combination of any 2 tubes. They can be the same tube or 2 different ones. For example: serrated and plane basket weave; No. 2 writing tubes; 2 shell (star) tubes; 2 serrated; or 2 plain basket weave tubes. There are many more combinations.

1. Fill the selected tubes with stiff peak white royal icing. The consistency is vital for optimum results. Be sure to never overfill your piping bag as this will result in bad pressure control and thereby give a lack of uniformity to the overall look.

2. Before commencing piping it is a good idea to mark out a grid on the cake to be decorated using a pin and ruler to ensure that even spaces are created throughout the design.

3. Commence by marking the icing with vertical lines according to the required width of the basket pattern using a pin.

4. Mark and pinprick the tube length on all the vertical lines from top to bottom of the cake. This ensures even spacing and straight lines when piping.

Basket Weave

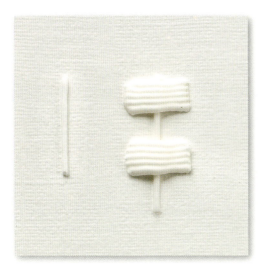

5. Using the No. 2 writing tube pipe the first vertical line exactly over the pin pricks from left to right if you are right-handed and right to left if left-handed.
6. Take the basket weave tube with the serrations on top and start to pipe from the top of the piped vertical line. Pipe 1 line horizontally which is equidistant on both sides of the central line.
7. Leave 1 tube width as per marked pinprick and pipe a second line across and down.
8. Repeat until you reach the bottom of the cake.
9. Pipe a second vertical line using the No. 2 writing tube starting at the top right hand side of the horizontal serrated line.

10. Holding the basket weave tube horizontally and applying even pressure, pipe a straight even line in between the first and second horizontal line until it meets the third marked vertical line.
11. A pattern is now forming which will be repetitive.
12. Pipe a third vertical line in the No. 2 writing tube and repeat the piping pattern forming a basket weave grid.

Assembly of Basket

The concept is to create a gift basket of flowers picked in a country garden setting.

1. A square double volume cake has been carved to form the angled square base for the basket. It follows pyramid angles which are inverted.

2. The cake is layered and filled, then covered with sugarpaste and left to dry.
3. Basket weave is piped all over the sides of the cake in royal icing and left to dry.
4. The dried basket weave is then coloured using a mixture of gold, yellow and brown using a sponge technique. It is later sprayed with confectioners glaze and left to dry.
5. The top trimming in rope work has been done using a clay gun and sugarpaste which is twisted onto itself and secured with Tylose glue. This adds a nice finishing touch to the edge of the basket.

Note

A neutral basket tone has been chosen to offset the beauty of the floral arrangement.

Tips

- When piping basket weave of any design, be careful not to push the tube in between the icing. Don't let the tube touch the icing - it is more advisable to let the icing fall into the space to be piped using good pressure control. This gives the design uniformity and even tension.
- It is also necessary to use an even pressure to pipe the lines.
- Do not start and stop as the piped work will not be uniform (similar to tension in knitting).

Romantic

String of Pearls

Leaves

1. Cut a ⅔ length of 33 gauge wire.
2. Hook the end tightly.
3. Roll varying size small balls of light green flower paste. Balls vary in size from 1mm-5mm in diameter.
4. Vein each ball with the textured end of a large cell stick and reshape into a ball.
5. Carefully pinch both ends of the balls to form points.
6. Using a scalpel or cutting blade slightly indent a line vertically down each ball of paste (pearl) to form the leaf and smooth over again.

Senecio Rowleyanus This is a creeping perennial succulent with cascading stems of large, round bead-like leaves. It is drought tolerant and native to South Africa. The bead-like foliage adds a decorative touch to hanging baskets and tropical gardens as well as cascading bridal bouquets. The pearl beads are in fact the leaves which are used in this arrangement.

Materials

Light green flower paste

Powder colours: snow, lime, emerald, lemon

Confectioners glaze

Isopropyl alcohol

Tylose glue

33 gauge wire

Modelling tools

Double white tissue

String of Pearls

7. Paint the hooked end of the wire with a little Tylose glue and thread the wire through the smallest pearl, pinching the end to secure it to the end of the wire.
8. Pinch the side to form a tiny stem.
9. Leave a small space and then paint a little Tylose glue on the wire where the next pearl is to be secured.
10. Thread the remaining pearls randomly at different angles along the wire gradually increasing their size. Random spacing must be left between the pearls.
11. Gently curve the wire as the threading progresses.
12. Leave the pearls to dry.
13. Mix snow and lemon powder colour with a little isopropyl alcohol and paint the wire between the pearls.
14. Mix a hint of emerald with lemon powder colour on a double white tissue and dust the pearls with a flat-ended dusting brush to deepen the shades. Steam very quickly over a pot of boiling water to set the colours.
15. Leave to dry.
16. Overdust with a hint of lime down the marked line. It must have a seamless transparent look.
17. Spray the string of pearls with concentrated confectioners glaze mixed with a ⅓ isopropyl alcohol.
18. Mix lemon and snow powder colours together on a double white tissue and dust the pearls with to achieve the speckled effect.
19. Leave to dry.

Tip

Silk thread can be used as an alternative to 33 gauge wire. The pearls can be threaded through using a needle and knotted between each one. Pearls can also be individually wired and taped onto a central stem.

   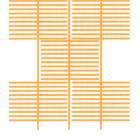

Basket Weave Template

Romantic 129

Assembly

This collection of country flowers has been arranged as a bridal bouquet suitable for a country-styled wedding.

The open champagne rose is dramatic in its delicate ivory/mocha shading with the white spider lilies adding a feeling of delicacy to the spray. The royal purple liriope is a complementary colour choice next to the orange ixora.

The fully-wired spray is also suitable to place in a basket or on a tall white cake which will show off the natural tones and muted shades to perfection.

If attaching the spray to a cake, a cell pick or posy pick should be used to insert the wire as the spray needs to cascade to present well.

The string of pearls helps to balance the cascading effect.

Serene

Ice white and cool blue colours give an air of calm to this beautiful bauhinia and periwinkle flower spray, while the dark shiny leaves add contrast.

The flower bouquet lies across the top of the cake, with oriental stringwork forming a decorative side border. Little blue periwinkle lace pieces complete the design.

Periwinkle

page 134

Bauhinia

page 137

Oriental stringwork

page 141

Periwinkle

Vinca Minor The periwinkle comes from North America, parts of Europe, China and India and is also known by the name of Vinca Minor vine. It is a shade-loving ground-cover with trailing stems. The flowers are blueish-lavender and it has dark green foliage with opposite glossy green leaves.

Materials

White flower paste

Powder colours: olive green, viridian, brown, lime, Barney, turquoise

28 gauge wire

Periwinkle cutter

Leaf cutter

Florist tape

Gardenia leaf former

Scalpel or hat-pin for scratching veins

Flowers

1. Shape a small ball of white flower paste into a teardrop shape. Flatten the bottom.
2. Using a small cell stick, roll the bottom part thinly, from the centre neck outwards.
3. Place a periwinkle cutter over the flattened cone shape and cut out.
4. Hollow out the centre with the sharp end of the cell stick.
5. Using a hat-pin, groove the middle of each petal to give a squared-off shape.
6. Pull a piece of 28 gauge wire through the centre of the flower and allow to dry.
7. Dust the petals a shade of Barney mixed with turquoise, leaving the middle and part of the inner edge of each petal white.
8. Paint the centre of the flower, deep in the middle, with a little yellow dot.

Tip

To keep the centre white place a little cotton wool or tissue down the centre of the flower while shading it. Remove when shading is complete.

Calyx

1. Take a small ball of light green paste and roll into a sausage shape.
2. Make a hole in the centre using the sharp end of a cell stick.
3. Cut the hollow sausage of paste into 4 leaving the base intact.
4. Using your fingers, twist and pull the 4 small sepals to elongate them, forming thin little strips which are pointed at the tips.
5. Dab a little water into the centre of the calyx with a fine paintbrush.
6. Push the back of the dried flower into the centre of the calyx, curving the sepals up the sides.

Buds

1. Take a small piece of white flower paste and form into a pointed teardrop shape. Groove the bud with a sharply pointed grooving tool to mark indents for the petals.
2. Dust the buds with a mix of Barney and turquoise and a little viridian mixed with brown.
3. Allow the bud to dry.
4. Make a calyx for the bud following the same method as used for the flower calyx and allow to dry.

Leaves

1. Roll out a piece of white flower paste, with a thickened ridge along the centre.
2. Insert a piece of 28 gauge wire into the thickened ridge.
3. Soften the edges with a balling tool.
4. Place the leaf onto a veiner to create the veins and markings.
5. Dry the leaf with a slight curve to the edge so that it is not completely flat.
6. Dust the leaf dark green, using a lighter green on the underside. To make a lighter shade of green mix in a little cornflour.
7. Use the point of a sharp scalpel to scratch veins into the leaf.
8. Steam, or spray with confectioners glaze, and allow to dry.

Flower Template

Leaf Template

Assembly

1. Tape 2 small leaves on either side of a bud placing the leaves directly opposite each other. Tape down the stem.
2. Tape 2 bigger leaves further down the stem. The leaves do not sit directly on the stem but have a piece of stalk before they meet the main stem.
3. Place a flower between the 2 leaves, also leaving a piece of stalk at the end of the flower before it joins the main stem.
4. Continue down the main stem creating a trailing vine.

Tips

- Make the leaves out of white flower paste and colour them using powder colours (mix shades of green together, such as viridian with a hint of brown, until you get the required leaf colour). Sift the powder colour through a fine strainer to blend the colours well before dusting. Note the underside of the leaf is paler than the upperside.
- Using the sharp end of a scalpel, scratch veins into the leaf following the lines created by the leaf veiner. Scratching removes the layer of colour and exposes the white of the paste underneath. The veins look far more realistic than if you were to paint them.
- Steam to set the colour.

Bauhinia

Stigma

1. Wrap a pea-sized ball of white flower paste around a piece of 24 gauge wire 7cm in length.
2. Work the paste down the length of the wire, covering the wire thinly on both ends but leaving a thickened piece ¾ of the way up.
3. While the paste is soft, bend the stigma into a gentle curve.
4. Flay the end of the stigma slightly with a sharp knife.

Bauhinia Variegata Alba Commonly called the Camel Foot tree or Butterfly tree, this plant originated in Hong Kong but is also grown extensively in India. The tree has large fragrant white flowers with lemon-green markings, similar to that of an orchid. The thickened stigma grows to form the pod as the flower dies. The tree usually flowers when it is bare of leaves then, as the pods start to form, the leaves sprout.

Materials

White flower paste
Powder colours: yellow, lime, viridian, emerald
Fine gelatine coloured pale yellow
Tylose glue
33, 28 & 24 gauge wire
No. 00 writing tube
Bauhinia petal cutter
Bauhinia leaf cutter
Bauhinia calyx cutter
Florist tape
Poppy veiner or grooving tool
Modelling tools

Bauhinia

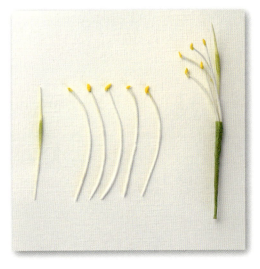  

Stamens

1. Use 5 pieces of 33 gauge wire, 5cm in length. As with the stigma, roll a small pea-sized ball of white flower paste over the length of the wire, coating as thinly and evenly as possible. Bend the stamens into a gentle curve.
2. Allow the stamens to dry.
3. Dip the tip of the dry stamen into Tylose glue and attach a tiny, slim piece of paste to the top to form the head of the stamen.
4. Brush with a little glue and dip into fine gelatine that has been coloured light brown/yellow using petal dust.

Assembly of the Stigma and Stamens

1. Colour the thickened pistol/stigma a mix of light lime/yellow.
2. Using florist tape, attach 3 of the stamens to the pistol, just slightly shorter in length. Check that they all bend in the same direction.
3. Attach the other 2 stamens slightly lower, also bending in the same direction. Secure well.

Labellum Petals

Labellum – also known as the lip or throat.

1. Roll out white flower paste thinly, leaving a thickened ridge in the centre (or use a grooved board).
2. Slide a 28 gauge wire through the middle of the thickened ridge at the base of the petal.
3. Vein slightly using a poppy veiner, and ball the edges to thin. Frill the petals slightly.
4. Fold the petal in half to create a central vein and allow to dry before colouring a line of light lime green from the base of the petal to ¾ of the way up.

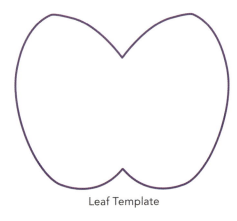

Leaf Template

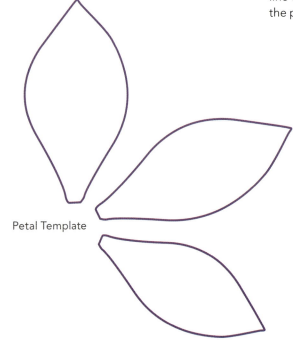

Petal Template

Calyx Template

138 Serene

Lateral Petals

1. Cut 2 petals using the same method as for the labellum. These petals are not frilly, so thin the edges and give a slight curve to the petal. Allow to dry before colouring with a small amount of yellow/lime colour at the base of the petal and halfway up the centre.

Assembly of the Flower

1. Attach the throat of the Bauhinia to the pistol and stamens that you wired up earlier, making sure that the stamens curve towards the throat of the flower.
2. Add the dorsal petals, 1 on either side of the throat, and tape securely.
3. The 2 lateral petals are slightly larger and sit above the 2 dorsal petals.
4. The flower has a significant gap between the 2 lateral petals.

Calyx

The flowers have a calyx that sits neatly in the gap between the lateral petals. It forms a crinkle at the base and as the flower ages the calyx browns and shrivels.

1. Cut the calyx and ball into a curve.
2. Dust to a medium leaf green using a mix of lime and yellow and wrap around the base of the flower.
3. Use a cell stick to shape the crinkle at the base.

Dorsal Petals

1. Cut 2 petals the same as the lateral petals. Allow to dry and colour in the same manner.

Buds

1. Roll a small ball of paste into a teardrop shape. The end is a thick point, not sharp.
2. Insert a 24 gauge wire at the thicker end and shape into a slight curve. Make grooves in the bud with a hat-pin or grooving tool.
3. Make several buds in varying sizes.
4. Leave the largest bud white and attach a green calyx, wrapping it around the bud neatly.

Leaves

1. Roll out pale leaf green paste leaving a thick ridge in the centre (or use a board with a groove).
2. Cut out the shape of the leaf and insert a 24 gauge wire into the thick ridge.
3. Soften the edges with a balling tool.
4. Fold the leaf in half to create a central vein.
5. Press the leaf onto a veiner (a dried leaf is just as effective).
6. Allow to dry.
7. Dust to a medium green (use viridian with a softer emerald to lighten).
8. Steam the leaf to set the colour and give it a sheen.

Note

The leaf stems and calyx are very similar in colour and should match each other.

Tip

To make stems look smooth use a cell stick and rub along the taped wire stems to even out uneven pieces of tape or wire. Use petal dust to colour stems so that they look realistic. We have used wire for the stamens, rather than using ready-made stamens, as the wire is able to bend.

Cake Board Design

The board has periwinkle cutouts.

1. Cover the cake board with white sugarpaste.
2. Mark even spacing around the board to fit the chosen design.
3. Take the periwinkle cutter and push it into the paste creating cut out sections. Do this while the paste is still soft.
4. Remove the cut out area by gently lifting away from the board.
5. Roll out periwinkle purple paste on a board and cut out the same amount of shapes as have been removed.
6. Insert coloured periwinkles into the cut out areas.
7. Over-pipe the cut out using a No. 00 writing tube and white royal icing.

Oriental stringwork

Oriental stringwork forms a decorative edge on the outer rim of a cake or a side design. In order to obtain the double-sided loops the cake is tipped upside down, therefore, this type of work is usually done on fruit cakes or dummy tiers.

Materials

Royal icing medium peak

Powder colours: Barney, turquoise

Piping bags

No. 0 & 00 writing tubes

Notes

- The outer sugar paste covering needs to have hardened sufficiently so that the cake does not mark or crack when overturned. It is advisable to turn the cake onto a soft towel or sponge.
- The composition of the design should complement the cake and be balanced.
- Oriental string work is decorative tube work. The loops are made with royal icing and a piping bag with either a No. 0 or 00 writing tube.
- The piping is executed directly onto the confectionary or cake using freshly made royal icing mixed to the correct consistency to suit the tube size.
- Consistent pressure will ensure even, neat and correctly formed loops.
- The pattern of the loops must be uniform.

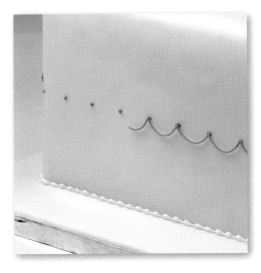 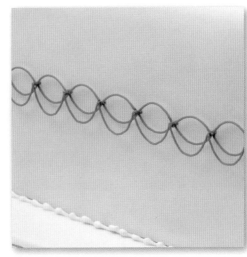 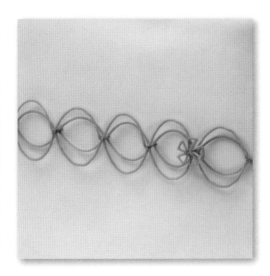

Method

1. Start the oriental tube-work with evenly spaced dots, piped at intervals along the side of the cake. The dots form the points where the loops meet and the joins should be neat.
2. Once the first row of loops has been executed, the cake is turned over and the second row of loops are piped, matching the first row exactly in size, length and shape.
3. Allow the first row to dry before turning the cake over.

5. Once the first 2 rows have been completed and allowed to dry, pipe a second small dot at the join and repeat the process using varied sizes of loops to create a pattern and 3D effect.
6. The overall product should be uniform. If piping along the edge of the cake make sure the cake is tipped onto something with a smaller diameter than the top of the cake.

Tips

- To help keep the loops straight and the same length, a line of masking tape stuck along the side of the cake will help. It will not leave a mark and it removes easily.
- Add 4 pinches of gum Arabic to a 2 egg mix of royal icing as it strengthens the mix. The tip of a teaspoon of liquid glucose will add stretch to the icing.

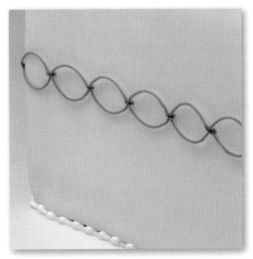

4. Different colours can be used to create interest and contrast.

Lace Point Template

Assembly

The flower arrangement is completely wired, however, no wires have pierced the icing or cake.

The arrangement has been attached to the top of the cake with a little royal icing.

The flower cutout has been outlined using a No. 00 writing tube and white royal icing. A bud, stem and piped leaf outline add interest and complete the design.

Stunning

Striking colours and distinctive finishing touches combine to make this design truly stunning.

The red sprekelia contrasts beautifully with the jade green of the bird flower giving a festive air to the cake. This cake would be perfect for a Christmas celebration or any other special occasion.

Sprekelia

page 146

Bird flower

page 149

Sugarpaste bows

page 153

Sprekelia

Sprekelia Formosissima Also known as Maltese Cross or Aztec Lily. This is a bulbous perennial lily native to Mexico and Guatemala. It flowers in late spring to early summer. The flowers are a striking crimson to scarlet colour, which add drama to any cake or floral arrangement. The soft blue green leaves are long and smooth, adding good contrast to a display. They are quite easy to make as the stamens and many of the petals can be made in advance and then put together as required.

Materials

White flower paste

Brown flower paste

Powder colours: x red, orange, ponceau, yellow, lime, brown

Tylose glue

28, 26, 24 & 22 gauge wire

Lily leaf cutter or template

Aztec lily templates or cutters

Pale green florist tape

Lily former

Modelling tools

Small pieces of foam

Foam ring or lily holder for drying petals and the lily

Stamens and Pistol

1. Colour a ball of flower paste scarlet red by mixing x red and orange.
2. Cut 6 pieces of 28 gauge wire 7cm in length and 1 piece 7.5cm in length.
3. Take a pea-sized piece of red flower paste and wrap it around the middle of a piece of wire.
4. Work the paste along the length of the wire using your fingers.
5. Roll the wire on a board or on a petal pad to make sure the wire is evenly and thinly coated, the thinner the better.
6. Do all 6 pieces in the same manner.
7. The pistol is slightly longer. Cover in the same manner as the stamens but allow a little paste to go over 1 end of the wire. Cut this piece into 3 to form the head of the pistol.
8. Place the pistol into the middle of the 6 stamens.
9. Tape the pistol and stamens to a piece of 22 gauge wire and secure well.
10. Bend the stamens and pistol into a gentle curve while the paste is still damp.
11. Top each stamen with a tiny anther made from light brown paste. Secure with glue and allow to dry.
12. Dust the base of the stamens green.

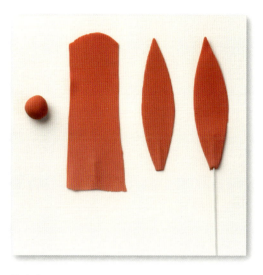

Petals

1. Roll out a piece of paste the same colour scarlet as used for the stamens.
2. Leave a ridge down the centre of the paste or use a grooved board.
3. Cut out 1 lily petal.
4. Use a former or veining tool to vein.
5. Fold the petal in half to create the central vein.
6. Wrap the petal around the base of the stamens with the stamens facing upwards.

7. Allow to dry over a curved former or roll, so the petal curves downwards in the opposite direction to the stamens.
8. Roll out a piece of paste using a grooved board or leave a thick ridge in the centre.
9. Cut out the second petal.
10. Slip a 26 gauge wire into the thickened part of the petal.
11. Ball the edges of the petal to thin using a large balling tool. Note: the petal is not very wavy.
12. Fold the petal down, shape into a gentle curve and allow to dry.
13. The third petal is cut and shaped in exactly the same way.
14. Once the petals are dry dust the base of each petal with a medium/light leaf green by mixing lime and yellow.
15. Dust the rest of the petal with x red, noting the tips of the petal are the lightest in colour.
16. Steam the petals to set the colour.
17. The 2 petals are attached on either side of the first petal and form a set of 3.
18. Tape together securely and put aside.

Petals (Top Set of 3)

1. Roll out flower paste using a grooved board or create a thickened ridge down the middle for a piece of 26 gauge wire.
2. Cut out 3 petals.
3. Ball the petals to thin the edges and soften into a gentle curve.
4. Vein using a lily veiner and fold each petal down the centre to create a deep middle vein.
5. Allow to dry.
6. Dust the base with a light to medium lime green to match the other 3 petals.
7. Dust the petals to the tips with x red and ponceau colour mixed together.
8. Steam to set.
9. Wire the 3 petals together so the middle petal is slightly longer than the other 2.

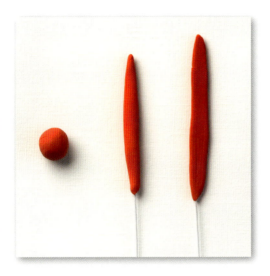

Assembly

1. The front 3 petals of this flower bend down almost at a right angle to the stem.
2. Attach the top 3 wired petals to the bottom 3.
3. Tape together securely.
4. The top 3 petals bend back and the stamens sit in the centre of the 2 halves.
5. Once the flower is complete, smooth the wire stem with a burnishing tool or cell stick and dust a lime.
6. The base of the flower has a thin piece of leaf attached which is the discarded calyx.
7. Roll out a thin piece of light brown paste.
8. Cut out a small leaf shape and vein with a grooving tool.
9. Dust light brown by mixing brown and cornflour.
10. Attach the leaf at the base of the flower.

Leaves

The leaves are slightly fleshy and slim in shape. They are long and pale green with fine narrow veins. The tip is thin and slightly rounded.

1. Shape a piece of paste into a sausage.
2. Roll to flatten, leaving a few centimetres at the base thicker so that a 24 gauge wire can be inserted almost ½ way up the leaf for support.
3. Cut out the leaf shape.
4. Soften the edges.
5. Vein on a veining mat.
6. Dust the top with lime and brown mixed together and use lime for the underside of the leaf.
7. Steam to set the colour and give the leaf a sheen.
8. Allow to dry.

Bud

1. Cut a ½ length piece of 24 gauge wire.
2. Roll a marble-sized piece of red paste into a cylinder shape, insert wire, then form a point and flatten the tip. The bud length is 7cm.
3. Use a knife or pin to groove the bud, indicating where the petals form. Vein the length of the bud. Cut the tip of the bud to form a new petal opening.
4. Roll out a small piece of light brown paste. Cut a small leaf shape. Vein with a Dresden tool. Ball the edges to thin.
5. Dust the petal with x red and orange and ponceau to match the petals of the flower. The base of the bud is a medium lime green colour.
6. Glue the brown leaf shape to the bottom of the bud to form a sheath. Allow to dry and then steam to set the colour.

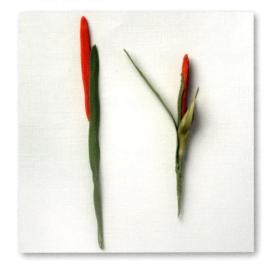

Bird Flower

Crotalaria Laburnifolia *This shrub can grow up to 3 metres high and grows in warm areas in full sun. The flowers look like small birds and the colour, a cross between mint green, lime green and jade, is quite unique.*

Making this flower out of icing is not as demanding as it looks – most of the small buds are shaped by hand and the open flowers can be done in stages and allowed to dry.

Materials

Flower paste

Powder colours: lime, emerald, violet, brown, viridian, lemon

Emerald and lemon mixed to a liquid colour

Tylose glue

24 & 20 gauge wire

Bird flower cutters

Leaf cutters for Bird flower

Veiners

Roller

A long hat pin

Flower drying stand

Modelling tools

Buds

The buds range in size from quite small to much larger. The smallest buds form at the bottom end of the vine.

1. Colour a large piece of flower paste pale lime green using emerald and lemon mixed together in a liquid as a base to work with.
2. Take a small piece of paste and form into a pea shape.
3. Shape one end of the pea into a tail.
4. Form the other end of the 'pea' into a head shape as seen in the photograph.
5. Insert a piece of 24 gauge wire that has been dipped into Tylose glue.
6. Elongate the tip of the head by working a little of the paste along the length of the wire as indicated to form a long beak.
7. Make several of these buds in the same manner ranging in size from the smallest (1cm) to the largest (2cm) in length.
8. Allow the buds to dry.
9. Dust the head of the bud and onto the 'beak' with a little light brown mixed with violet.
10. Dust the side of the bud with a mix of lime and viridian to add colour and life to the buds.
11. Steam to set the colour and allow to dry.

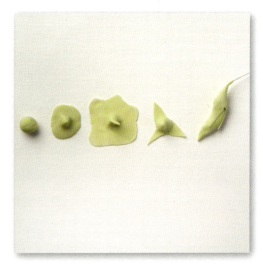

Larger Buds

The larger buds have small lateral petals with the hood of the flower becoming more predominant.

Part One

1. Make a bud as per previous instructions. The size needs to be approx 2.5cm in length.
2. Do not shape the head, but bring the body to a point and stop. The middle needs to be nice and rounded.
3. Roll out a thin piece of green paste.
4. Cut out 2 wing shapes.

5. Ball the edges to thin.
6. Vein with a grooving tool.
7. Attach the petals on either side of the body of the flower.
8. Allow to dry.
9. Dust the petals with lime and the smaller petals on the sides with a touch of viridian and violet.

10. Dust the tip of the tail with violet and light brown.

Part Two

11. Take a piece of paste the size of a small marble.
12. Form the ball into the shape of a Mexican hat (witch's hat).
13. Roll the paste flat around the base.
14. Using the template or cutter, cut out the hood shape.
15. Make sure the thick part is in the middle of the triangle.
16. Insert a piece of 24 gauge wire with a hook on the end into the thick part of the 'head'.
17. Work a little paste up the wire to form the beak.
18. Hollow out head of the flower.
19. Wet the hood with Tylose glue.
20. Push the hood over the top of the body of the flower.
21. Work into position and allow to dry.
22. Dust the hood of the flower with violet and brown.
23. Steam the bud and allow to dry.

Note

Make several larger buds in the same manner. The bodies can all be made in advance and allowed to dry, with the side petals attached and the hoods placed at a later stage.

Open Flower

1. Roll out a piece of lime green paste ensuring the paste is not too thin.
2. Cut out the body shape using the flower cutter.
3. Allow the shape to dry slightly.
4. Ball out the middle of each side to create a bulge.
5. Fold the body in half and join the edges with a little glue.
6. Insert a piece of 24 gauge wire where the top of the 2 petals join. Secure well.
7. Join the edges carefully without flattening the bulge in the middle. The shape of the flower is like a green pea.
8. Allow to dry and colour in the same manner as the larger buds.
9. Attach the 2 petals on either side of the body in the same way as you prepared the larger bud.
10. Dust with powder colour to match.

The open flower has a petal which forms a cape.

1. Roll out lime green paste and cut out 1 'cape' shape using template provided.
2. Ball the cape along the edges to thin.
3. Vein the petal with a grooving tool.
4. Using a small balling tool, ball just inside the edge to form a ridge all the way around the petal.
5. Fold the petal in half to create a central vein.
6. Attach the petal at the point onto the body of the flower with a little glue.

As the flower ages, the petal that forms the cape curls up over the back of the body so make some flowers with the cape lying flat and others curled up over the hood of the flower.

1. Use a piece of foam to hold the petal in a curled position until it dries.
2. To complete the open flower, dust with a mix of lime, emerald and viridian to add depth to the flower. The tail, beak and hood is brown/violet in colour.
3. Steam to set and give the flower a final sheen.

Assembly

1. Take a 20 gauge wire and cover the length with light green florist tape.
2. Tape the smallest bud, the beak side to the main stem, at one end of the wire.
3. Continue down the main stem, attaching buds from the smallest size to the biggest and then the open flowers.

Pod

As the flower ages, the colour of the flower turns a more yellow/lime green. A pod begins to form in the centre of the flower. As the petals drop, the pod becomes a small pea once again, but it has a very curly tail.

The small pea is attached to the hood of the flower, and continues to grow and then ripen, turning from green to brown and finally dropping its seeds on the forest floor. The pod has not been used in the arrangement.

Leaves

The leaves are attached to a woody stem. Tiny leaves form at the apex of the stem and graduate from small to large. The leaves form in a set of 3 with the middle leaf slightly larger in size. The leaves are slightly more cupped on 1 side, rather than completely flat. The leaves have strong veins so a gardenia veiner works well as a leaf former.

The same method is used for all 5 sizes of leaf.

1. Use a ball of light leaf green paste as a base and colour to a deeper green when the leaves are dry.
2. Take a small marble-sized piece of paste.
3. Roll on a grooved board or roll out the paste leaving a thicker ridge in the centre.
4. Cut out 1 leaf shape using a cutter or the template provided.
5. Dip a piece of 24 gauge wire into Tylose glue and slip into the ridge, taking care not to break through the flower paste.
6. Use a large balling tol thin the edges.
7. Press the leaf shape into a former and allow to dry.
8. Once the leaf is dry dust with a mix of viridian and brown to achieve the correct shade.
9. Use a mix of x green, lime and brown to achieve the correct shade.
10. Steam to set the colour.
11. When dry, arrange the leaves in a bract of 3.
12. Tape the leaves to the main stem. The tip of the stem has a cluster of small leaves with the larger leaves at the bottom of the main stem.

Tips

- A 20 gauge wire has been used for the main stem as it is sturdy.
- Use a burnishing tool to smooth the wire and colour the stem with dusting powder to make it look as natural as possible.
- Use the back of a gardenia leaf if you don't have a specific veiner for this unusual species.

Leaf Template

Sugarpaste Bows

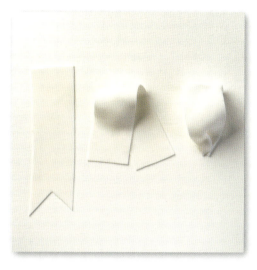

Method

1. Roll out a piece of sugarpaste as thinly as possible.
2. Cut 4 pieces the same width (if you have a good size ruler, the width of the ruler is very useful as the size will be uniform when cutting the strips).
3. When the lengths of paste have been cut, cut a V shape on one end of each tail. Make 1 ribbon slightly shorter than the other.

Sugarpaste bows add form and structure to a cake and are a great filler when used with flowers that are made from flower paste. Bows can be dusted with a lustre colour, embossed or decorated with a piped design. The ribbon on this cake adds a sense of drama as it is detailed with a modern design piped in black. It also complements the scarlet coloured sprekelia.

Materials

Sugarpaste

Black royal icing medium peak (refer royal icing section)

Ruler

Modelling tools

No. 0 or 1 writing tube

Cotton wool, cloud or foam

Sugarpaste Bows

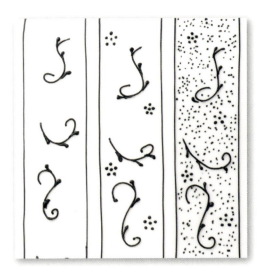  

4. Before the paste dries, pipe the design onto the ribbon tails.

5. Use a No. 0 or 1 writing tube for piping the pattern onto the cake.

6. Allow the 2 tails of ribbon to dry with a slight curve and fold so that it looks like real fabric.

7. Bend the other 2 pieces of paste into loops.

8. Dry the loops with a little foam in the centre to hold the shape, or simply lie the loop on its side to dry.

9. Once the loops are dry, pipe on the same pattern.

Tips

- Wire can be added to the tails and loops should you wish to use the ribbon as part of the arrangement.
- The cake design has ribbon that crosses over the top of the tiers similar to a parcel. The strips of ribbon are decorated with the same design as the bows. The piped design has been used to add depth and texture to the ribbon.
- The ribbon in the arrangement and on the cake is not wired but simply pushed into place while still pliable, then fixed with a little royal icing.
- When making a bow keep the ribbon tails the same width as the loops.
- The size of the bow needs to be in keeping with the size of the cake and the flowers used in the arrangement.

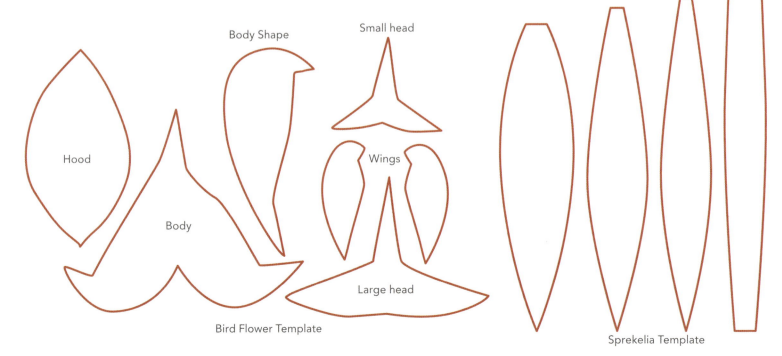

Assembly

The flowers have been wired into two individual sprays, one smaller than the other, then placed separately on opposite corners of the two-tiered cake.

The sugarpaste bows have been added to each spray and arranged so they 'fall' naturally down the side of the cake and onto the board.

Vibrant

Vibrant red, lush green and classic white colour tones ensure this cake makes an impact whatever the occasion. The spectacular floral arrangement is displayed against an 'inverted comma' shaped cake and finished with delicate lace point highlights.

Poinciana

page 158

Sword fern

page 161

Russelia 'lemon falls'

page 162

St. Joseph lily

page 164

Lace points

page 168

Poinciana

Stamens

1. Tape 9 full length white stamens to a ¼ length 30 gauge wire. The tenth stamen is a little longer than the rest.
2. Paint all stamens with x red. Gently curl 9 of them forwards and the longer one backwards.
3. Paint the tips with Tylose glue and then dip them in rust coloured pollen.

Delonix Regia The poinciana is a deciduous tree native to Madagascar. It grows up to 15m tall and has been naturalised in Western Australia. The flower petals are scarlet red in colour and are approximately 8cm long.

Materials

White flower paste

Powder colours: x red, yellow, orange, snow, rubine, lime, brown

Rust pollen

Confectioners glaze

Tylose glue

Isopropyl alcohol

33, 30 & 24 gauge wire

White fine stamens

Poinciana cutters

Large poppy veiner

Toothpick

Double white tissue

Modelling tools

Petals

1. There are 5 petals in total – 4 plain scarlet red petals and 1 standard upright petal, with red on one side and white and yellow marked with reddish brown striped flecks on the other side.
2. Cut 5 x ⅓ length 30 gauge wires.
3. Cut out 2 petal shapes in white flower paste. Thin the edges with a large balling tool but do not frill at this stage.
4. Place 1 petal the wrong side up and paint a stripe of Tylose glue from the top to the bottom of the petal leaving 5mm at the top of the flower. Place the cut wire on top of the glue. Then place the second petal shape on top of the first. Stroke down with the finger.
5. Place the small cell stick adjacent to the central wire and thin on ether side of the petal stretching it dramatically. Do not roll over the central wire as this will cause the paste to rip open.
6. Re-cut with original size cutter.
7. Vein with poppy veiner and frill the upper edges on a hard rolling mat using a small cell stick.
8. Place on a double white tissue and dust with orange, then overdust with x red.
9. Give the stem a gentle movement backwards and steam to set colour (steaming is optional).
10. Repeat this process with the 3 remaining red petals.
11. For the fifth petal, repeat the process and dust 1 side red. Next, turn the petal over and dust this side with a mixture of snow powder colour and cornflour. Ball with a large balling tool from the neck to the tip of the petal. Be careful not to smudge the white side with excess red. Dust the base ¼ of the way up with yellow. Steam. With a fine paintbrush or toothpick, paint rubine fleck lines.

Assembly

1. Tape the petals around the stamens neatly in a circular formation. Tape the white petal facing upwards towards the stamens.

Calyx

1. Cut out 1 flower calyx shape in moss green (mix lime and brown powder colours together) flower paste. The paste should be thin, but not too thin, as the calyx is fleshy.
2. Ball gently to thin the edges and stretch a little in size.
3. Paint 1 side with yellow mixed with isopropyl alcohol and the other side with x red and isopropyl alcohol.
4. Paint the base of the flower with Tylose glue and feed the calyx up the wire to reach the base of the flower. Secure gently in the middle only.

Buds

1. Take a pea-sized ball of light moss green flower paste and insert a hooked 24 gauge wire by burning it into the paste.
2. Overdust with yellow and then lime.
3. Mark 3 lines down the bud. Paint with a hint of x red in the lined area.
4. Steam, let dry and then tape with light green florist tape.

Leaves

The leaves, which have hundreds of miniature leaf bracts, are not often made in flower paste as they are very time-consuming to make.

1. Using the smallest calyx cutter make many green leaves by inserting 33 gauge wire.
2. Dust with a lime and then dip in 50/50 confectioners glaze/isopropyl alcohol mix.
3. Tape each one individually with Nile green florist tape, then tape them down the stem. Start with 1 at the top and then tape in pairs opposite one another.

Tips

- Steam petals over a boiling pot or kettle for a few seconds only. This sets and deepens the colour.
- Burning wire into the paste causes crystallisation of the sugar and immediate adhesion.
- By fully wiring the flower petals there is less chance of breakage. It is easier to obtain more movement and assemble the flower when it is slightly wet.

Note

As the flower ages, the standard upright petal changes its colour. When it opens, the bud is a peach shade. This changes to white when the flower is fully open. Finally, when the flower is at its largest, it changes to yellow.

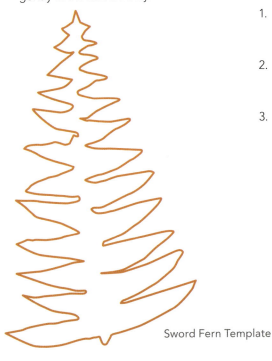

Sword Fern Template

Calyx Template

Petal Template

Sword Fern

Polystichum munitum Named after its saw-toothed leaflets the sword fern is evergreen and resistant to weather changes. Its understated foliage makes a huge impact and works well with most floral arrangements.

Materials

Light green flower paste

Powder colours: yellow, brown, lime, viridian

Tylose glue

Confectioners glaze in a spray bottle

28 gauge wire

Sword fern cutter

Sword fern veiner

Modelling tools

Light green florist tape

Method

1. Cut ½ length 28 gauge wire.
2. Roll light lime green paste very thinly onto the wire and gently curve.
3. Cut out 1 sword fern shape and thin the edges on a balling mat.
4. Place a thin strip of Tylose glue down the back of the leaf and place the covered wire on top of the glue.
5. Vein with the fern veiner by gently pressing paste between the mould.
6. Shade with yellow and then lime. Overdust with a little brown and finally viridian.
7. Gently bend the leaf shape in the direction you want the movement of the leaf.
8. Spray with a 50/50 mixture of isopropyl alcohol and confectioners glaze and leave upright to dry.
9. Tape with light green florist tape.

Tip

When using plastic cutters that may be slightly worn on the edges a clean cut can be achieved by sliding the cutter and paste off the edge of the board. This also works when a cutter has a lot of detail which may not be easy to cut out in paste.

Russelia 'Lemon Falls'

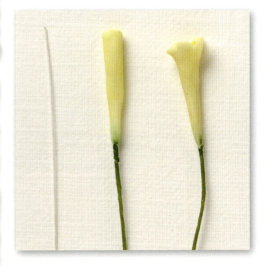

Russelia Equisetiformis This shrub is native to Mexico and has slender, green branching stems and cascading tubular lemon flowers measuring approximately 2.5cm in length. The flowers are also found in red. Their cascading elegance makes a spectacular display and provide a delicate undertone in floral arrangements.

Materials

White flower paste
Powder colours: lemon, lime
Tylose glue
33 & 28 gauge wire
Superfine seed head white stamens
Small 5 petal round blossom cutter
Light green florist tape
Modelling tools

Flower

1. Cut ¼ length 33 gauge wire and hook the end tightly.
2. Roll out a tiny ½ pea-sized ball of white flower paste into a sausage shape measuring around 2.5cm long and flatten the bottom against a hard surface.
3. Use the end of a paintbrush which has been dipped in cornflour to prevent sticking and roll out a witch's hat from the flattened base. Make sure it is extremely thin.
4. Place a blossom cutter over the sausage shaped piece of paste and cut out 1 shape.
5. Hold the shape between the fingers. Using the small cell stick indent the centre and squeeze gently against the fingers.
6. Take a small sock needle and dust it with cornflour. Push the needle down the centre of the flower to form a trumpet shape and hollow it out.
7. Paint a little Tylose glue on the hooked wire and feed it halfway down the centre of the flower squeezing the paste against the wire as it reaches the bottom. Roll between the fingers to make an evenly-rounded base.

Russelia 'Lemon Falls'

 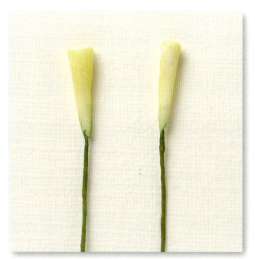 

8. Colour the heads of the seed head stamens lemon by laying them on a double white tissue and dusting with a flat-ended dusting brush.
9. Cut 5 stamens 1.5cm long and place them all down the centre of the flower. It is best to do so when the flower is still wet as they will adhere to the wet paste and will not require glue to hold them in place.
10. Mark fine indents down the trumpet of the flower using a Dresden or veining tool.
11. Dust the flower all over with lemon.
12. Leave to dry.

Buds

Make many buds in varying sizes as there are at least 5 buds, in different stages, per sprig.

1. Cut ¼ length 33 gauge wire and hook the end.
2. Paint the hooked end with Tylose glue.
3. Roll out white flower paste in varying sizes – from ½ pea-sized to pinhead-sized – and insert the wire into the paste.
4. Roll paste down the wire to form a teardrop shape.
5. Mark 2 lines which cross over one another on top of the teardrop shape.
6. Dust with lemon using a little lime mixed with lemon at the base. This forms a very new bud.
7. For slightly more mature buds hollow out a tiny area and make 4 cuts in the circumference area to form 5 petals.
8. Place the cell stick into the slightly hollowed area and squeeze against cell stick to thin.
9. Shade the same.

Leaves

Leaves are fairly insignificant but form short twig like formations as described in the assembly below.

Assembly

1. Cut ¼ length wire and tape with light green florist tape.
2. Leave 2cm. Tape in a bud and then continue to tape at staggered intervals varying the size of the buds and flowers.
3. Tape in varying lengths of wire covered with light green florist tape or paste between each flower (for show work you would use paste not tape).
4. Tape onto a 28 gauge wire for length and support.

Flower Template

St. Joseph Lily

Lilum candidum of the plant genus **Hippeastrum.** This flower is named after St. Joseph, spouse of Mary, and the translated meaning is pure and upright – as typified in the flower's growth.

Some artistic license has been used in the sizing of the St. Joseph lily as the real lily would be far too large to place on a cake.

Materials

White flower paste

Light green flower paste

Powder colours: pearl, lime, lemon, yellow, viridian, emerald

Tylose glue

Cornflour

33, 30, 28 & 20 gauge wire

St. Joseph lily cutters

Light green florist tape

Silicone lily tepal veiner

Palm frond section

Double white tissue

Bubble sponge

Modelling tools

Centre Stamens

1. Cut 6 x ½ lengths of 33 gauge wire.
2. Roll pieces of white flower paste onto the wires to cover – covered area should be ⅔ of the size of the cutter you are using.
3. Take the covered wire and roll out on a board using a small metal roller or cell stick. Cut down the sides of the wire and then smoothly re-roll on a rolling mat or between the palm of the hands. The stamens must have a smooth and thin finish to them and must all be the same thickness and length.
4. Repeat the process with the remaining 5 wires.
5. Make sure all the lengths of covered stamens are even. If required pinch the bottoms to make them the same.
6. Give the stamens a gentle curve by stroking them between the thumb and forefinger.
7. Mix some cornflour with a little emerald mixed with lemon to make a very light green shade. Lay the stamens on a double white tissue and dust with the colour mixture. For a realistic shade it must be barely green.

Tip

Keep the lengths of the stamens equal. This gives balance when assembling the flower.

Anthers

1. Using white flower paste, roll 6 very tiny sausages measuring 5mm length x 1mm depth (anthers have been scaled down in size).
2. Take the coloured stamens and paint the tips with a little Tylose glue. Firmly place the small rolled pieces of paste (anthers) on top of stamen filament.
3. Leave to dry a little.
4. To make the pollen, mix fine gelatine with yellow, orange and a hint of brown to form a rust coloured powder and shake well in a lidded container. This can be any colour you wish but in the case of the lily it is usually yellow, violet or rust colour.
5. Paint the anthers with a little Tylose glue and dip in pollen mixture. Alternatively, a less messy method is to apply a little petal base to the anthers and then dip them in the pollen mixture.

Tip

When making the anthers always use ½ the amount of paste you start with. Be sure to roll it extremely thinly and use very little Tylose glue as when you apply the pollen it thickens the anther size dramatically, which can leave the anther looking chunky and out of proportion.

Pistol

1. Cut a ½ length 30 gauge wire. Roll a sausage of white flower paste a little thicker than the stamens and a little longer than the length of the lily cutter.
2. Repeat the thinning out procedure as described in making the stamens.
3. Thicken 1.5cm up the base of the pistol by rolling on a little more flower paste. Make sure there are no cracks and that joins are invisible. This forms the ovary.
4. Dust the same green shade.

5. Roll out a small pea-sized ball of white flower paste and mark three lines on the top and down the side in a 'peace sign' or triangular formation.
6. Dust with a little pearl lustre mixed with a hint of emerald. This forms the stigma.
7. Glue the ball (stigma) on to the top of the pistol with a little Tylose glue.

Lace Point Template

St. Joseph Lily

Assembly

1. Cut a long length of ¼ width Nile green florist tape and tape all 6 stamens together with the curve going outward.
2. The stamens must be taped one by one otherwise the correct balance will not be achieved. Should the stamens move around a little, tape approximately 2.5cm down to secure the placing of the stamens and then tape up to the top again.
3. Tape neatly and evenly, making sure that the base of the stamens all meet.

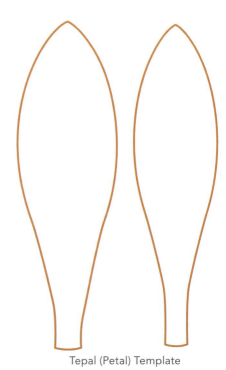

Tepal (Petal) Template

Tepals (Petals)

There are 6 tepals to the lily. Some lilies, like the St. Joseph lily, have 3 small and 3 large tepals.

1. Cut out 3 large and 3 small tepals and place them under a damp cloth which is sealed in a plastic zip lock bag. This will slow down the drying process. The tepals must be rolled on a grooved board to create the centre vein.
2. Cut 6 x ½ length pieces of 28 gauge wire.
3. Insert 1 piece of wire into each lily tepal about ⅔ of the way up.
4. Vein with a lily tepal veiner.
5. Place the tepals on a double white tissue and dust with a mixture of pearl, snow and cornflour. Finally dust the base and up the back central vein with the green pearl mixture that you used to dust the stamens. Dust all 6 tepals on both sides.
6. Place on balling mat and gently thin the edges giving a little movement to the petal.
7. Gently curve the upper ½ of each tepal between the thumb and forefinger so that it curves outwards a little.

Tip

Keep the tepals under a damp cloth which has been placed inside a zip lock plastic bag until they have all been made and are ready to dust, shape and tape together. This way, when assembling the flower, the paste looks almost fused at the bottom as it does in nature.

Assembly

1. Take the taped stamen centre and tape 1 large petal and then 1 small petal overlapping one another around the stamens. Repeat the process until all 6 tepals have been taped.
2. Tape to the end of the wires.
3. With the lily upside down, gently squeeze the base of the petals together and then shape into a closed or open lily.
4. The flower shade can be adjusted once the whole flower is assembled.
5. Dust the outside flower base a little deeper with the green shading used previously in the centre of the flower and for the stamens.

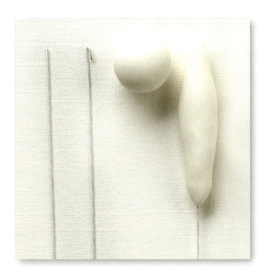  

Bud

1. Roll a ball of paste proportional to the flower size into a long tapered bud leaving the base a little rounded.
2. Mark 3 grooves downwards from top to bottom of the bud. Insert a hooked 20 gauge wire by burning it into the paste. This causes crystallisation of the sugar particles and immediately adheres the paste to the wire.

Leaves

The leaves are long and fairly thin in formation.

1. Colour some white flower paste light emerald green.
2. Cut 28 gauge wire into half lengths.
3. Thinly roll out green paste into a long shape on the board.
4. Paint the wire with Tylose glue and place on the bottom half of the rolled out paste.
5. Fold the top half of the paste over the bottom half and roll over with the small rolling pin or cell stick.
6. Using a cutting wheel cut out a long thin leaf shape, which is thicker in the middle.
7. Pinch the top and mark a central vein down the middle.
8. Vein on a piece of palm frond or with a lily leaf veiner.
9. Thin the edges on the balling mat to create movement.
10. Dust the leaf all over with yellow, then use emerald followed by a little lime. Finally finish by dusting a little viridian or x green at the base and down the central vein of the leaf.
11. Spray with a 50/50 mixture of confectioners glaze and isopropyl alcohol. Leave to dry on a bubble sponge. When the leaf is almost dry curve it gently backwards, then leave to dry completely.

3. Cut the top of the bud into 3 sections by snipping down, about 5mm only, with fine embroidery scissors. Gently pinch the snipped pieces together. This forms an opening bud.
4. Shade with pearl and lime at the base and intermittently blend through to the top of the bud.
5. Tape with green florist tape all the way down the stem.

Leaf Template

Lace Points

Lace points add a decorative finishing touch to the edge of the cake. They are piped with royal icing using No. 1, 0 or 00 writing tubes. The pattern of the lace should complement the cake design.

Materials

Royal icing (refer royal icing section)
Petal base (solidified vegetable oil)
Acetate paper
Perspex or glass sheet
No. 1 writing tube
Piping bag

Method

1. Cut a sheet of acetate paper or cellophane the size of the Perspex or glass sheet being used.
2. Spread petal base all over the glass sheet.
3. Lay acetate paper on top of glass. This sticks acetate to the piece of glass and is easily removed.
4. Place the lace pattern underneath the acetate.
5. Use a No. 1 writing tube to pipe the lace piece pattern on the acetate. The dots should not have peaks and the joins in the piped lines should not be visible.
6. Leave to dry completely overnight.
7. Remove lace points from the acetate sheet by using a flat trowel. Handle with extreme care. Use of a toothpick enables easy handling.
8. Secure on cake or design using a tiny dot of royal icing which is not visible when the points are attached.

Note

Lace points must always be complementary to the design of the cake.

Tips

- Acetate allows the lace points to be lifted off the glass sheet easily when dried and does not require direct contact with the petal base or fat.
- Petal base will weaken royal icing and could cause grease marks on a cake if used in excess.

Assembly

This unusal modern design is easily achievable as the heaviest part of the cake is at the bottom. Cover the top side of the cake in sugarpaste (cut out a template using the pan the cake was baked in as a guide) and allow to dry. Turn the cake over and cover the remaining three sides with sugarpaste. Use a cotton wool ball to dust the cake with pearl lustre, followed by lemon, then apricot. The spray is attached to the cake using royal icing. Lace points have been chosen to complement the design of the cake and finish the edges. They have also been attached using a little royal icing.

Royal Icing

Royal icing has many applications and is used to pipe both base and side borders, to make piped flowers, in flood work or run-in work, calligraphy, lace points, filigree, brush embroidery and more. It is also the basic ingredient in flower paste, which is used to make beautiful fine-modelled flowers.

Ingredients
1 egg white at room temperature

Approx 300-400g (depending on size of egg white) sifted icing sugar mix or pure icing sugar sifted through organza

Actiwhite

Pinch cream of tartar

¼ tsp liquid glucose or Gum Arabic for strength

Materials
Small glass bowl

Small metal spatula

Miniature whisk

Royal icing is made from a mixture of egg white, icing sugar and air which is beaten together well. Egg white has a PH of 8 and needs to be neutralised for optimum efficiency. Therefore, acid is added. Acid can be found in varying forms: lemon juice, white vinegar, cream of tartar or acetic acid, however, acetic acid is not entirely edible and therefore not often used. Lemon juice can weaken and discolour the egg white so a very fine grain cream of tartar is the most effective. Other ingredients may be added as described in this chapter.

Optimum results require room temperature.

Method
1. Place the egg white in a small glass bowl. (Do not use a plastic bowl as plastic is porous and fat molecules adhere to it which break down the royal icing.)
2. Use a miniature whisk to gently break up the egg white.
3. Add a pinch of cream of tartar and ¼ teaspoon of Actiwhite or Pavlova mix and ¼ tsp liquid glucose (to give extra strength).
4. Continue to whisk by hand until well blended.
5. Add the icing sugar ½ tsp at a time and continue to beat in well until fully blended. If too much icing sugar is added at one time the icing becomes thick and heavy and the proportions of air, icing sugar and egg white are imbalanced.
6. Continue whisking in the icing sugar until a medium peak forms. (You will have to change to mixing with a spatula or a knife at this stage as the icing becomes too heavy for the miniature hand whisk.)
7. Depending on the work being completed, a soft, medium or stiff peak royal icing is required.
8. The quantity of icing sugar needed for correct consistency depends on the size of the egg white used.
9. Once the correct consistency has been reached, cover with plastic wrap and a damp cloth.

Soft Peak

The peak falls down easily but keeps its shape. This consistency is used for flood work, pressure piping, brush embroidery and piping dots.

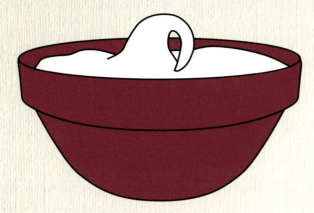

Medium Peak

The peak must remain lifted with only the very top falling over slowly.

Stiff/Firm Peak

The top of the peak must not fall down at all. When touching the icing with a finger it will only just leave a trace on the finger.

Different Consistencies

There are 3 different consistencies which are used for various applications: stiff, medium and soft peak. It is essential that the correct consistency is achieved for each particular type of work to ensure success.

To check consistency

- Wipe the spatula clean.
- Dip the clean spatula in the royal icing and gently lift to form a peak.
- If the peak falls down easily but keeps its shape then this is soft peak consistency.
- Medium peak means a peak forms at the top of the icing that gently curves over but does not stay upright.
- Stiff/Firm peak is when the top of the icing forms a peak that holds its shape and doesn't fall down at all.

Recipe for Actiwhite Royal Icing

1. Mix 10g of Actiwhite with 80ml of warm water. Let it stand for 15 minutes.
2. Beat in sifted icing sugar until the required consistency is achieved.

Tips

- Add 5ml liquid glucose and 2.5ml Gum Arabic to 1 egg white mix of royal icing. Approximately 300-400mg icing sugar is used.
- Actiwhite acts as a volumiser in making royal icing.
- If royal icing has been left for more than an hour always make sure that you beat it well before using it. Do not make the mistake of adding more icing sugar if you think it is too runny as it will dry out too quickly and become heavy.
- Depending on location and the increased humidity in the atmosphere in some areas, icing sugar mix may be a better option and still has the required strength but can lose its gloss. Fewer sugar crystals are formed in comparison to pure icing sugar.
- Should you be gluten intolerant then pure icing sugar is preferable, however, there is a gluten free mix available.

Snail Trail Border

This is the most frequent of piping techniques used. This border has been used on most of the cakes in this book.

To pipe a snail trail, medium peak consistency is required.

1. Place a small amount (1tbs) royal icing in piping bag which has a writing tube placed inside.
2. Hold the bag at a 40° angle and pipe a ball using even pressure.
3. When the required size of the ball is achieved, gradually ease off the pressure and touch the board to form a tail. The end result looks like a tadpole or teardrop.
4. Start the next shape 1mm away from the end of the tail and continue the pattern using the same amount of pressure as before and keeping the shapes all uniform. There should be no gaps in the border.

Dots

Soft to medium peak royal icing must be used.

1. Cut the end of a piping bag to allow space for the nozzle.
2. Place a writing tube inside the piping bag and fill with a little royal icing.
3. Hold the bag just off an angle of 90° and apply slow even pressure to build up the size of the dot required. When removing the nozzle from the icing always take it away gently from a sideways angle so no peaks are formed at the top.

Note

Dots must always be well rounded and have a full-bodied formation.

Tip

- A few drops of glycerine can be added to slow down the drying process and prevent peaks from forming.
- If peaks are visible, immediately pat them down with the end of a fine dry paintbrush.
- Good pressure control makes good dots.

Recipe Collection

These are tried and tested recipes – collected over the years and passed from teacher to demonstrator. We have changed some of them for personal use and tweaked them to suit our individual baking and decorating requirements.

Standard metric measurements are used in all recipes.

Coffee Walnut Cake

Ingredients

180g plain flour

20ml baking powder

1ml salt

100g finely chopped walnuts

4 egg yolks

200g white sugar

125ml sunflower oil

5ml vanilla essence

10ml instant coffee dissolved in 125ml boiling water

4 jumbo egg whites

Method

1. Sift flour with 15ml of baking powder and salt.
2. Add walnuts.
3. Whip egg yolks in a separate bowl until creamy then slowly add sugar, whisking all the time until doubled in volume.
4. Add oil, vanilla essence and dissolved coffee.
5. Whisk until all ingredients are well mixed.
6. In a third bowl, whisk egg whites till stiff and then add remaining baking powder and whisk again.
7. Add egg yolk mixture to flour mixture and FOLD in slowly.
8. Add egg white mixture and FOLD in thoroughly.
9. Pour into 20cm round cake pan and bake at 170°C for approx 1 hour.
10. When firm to the touch take out of oven and turn onto a wire rack to cool.
11. Fill with a coffee flavoured butter icing.

Chocolate Cake

Ingredients

1¾ cups self raising flour

1½ cups sugar

½ cup cocoa

¾ cup hot water

½ tsp baking powder

3 extra large egg yolks
(4 if not extra large)

½ cup oil

Pinch of salt

Optional

1 cup of melted couveture chocolate can be added for a richer flavour.

Method

1. Mix flour and sugar together.
2. Mix cocoa, hot water and salt together in a separate bowl.
3. Mix cocoa mixture, egg yolks and oil together (add optional chocolate).
4. Fold flour mixture into cocoa mixture.
5. Add another ½ cup water, brandy or orange juice.
6. Beat egg whites with ½ tsp baking powder until stiff.
7. Fold egg whites into cocoa mixture and make sure mixture is well blended.
8. Bake at 170°C for about 45 minutes. The baking time will depend on your oven and size of cake. Listen to the cake, when you can smell it and it is firm to the touch, remove from the oven, turn out of cake tin and allow the cake to cool on a wire rack.

Notes

- Divide into 3 layers and sandwich with white or dark chocolate ganache.
- If chocolate has been folded into the cake put a cup of water in the oven to keep the air moist and prevent crusting on the top of the cake.
- This cake improves in taste after 24 hours and freezes well.

Chocolate Cream Cheese Cake

Ingredients

For the filling

2 x 250ml packets Philadelphia cream cheese

500ml cream

250g couveture chocolate (white, milk or dark)

3 tsp (15ml) gelatine dissolved (optional)

For the base

1 packet of digestive biscuits

150g ground hazelnuts

100ml (¼ cup) brown sugar

100g butter (melted)

Method

1. Crush the biscuits very finely in a blender and add the melted butter, hazelnuts and brown sugar. Combine thoroughly.
2. Grease a 23cm spring-form cake tin and pack in the biscuit base. Put in the refrigerator to set for 30 minutes.
3. Mix together all the remaining ingredients thoroughly (add the melted chocolate and gelatine last).
4. Pour onto the prepared biscuit base and leave to set in fridge a couple of hours.
5. Remove from the tin and decorate according to chosen design.

Notes

- ml does not = mg.
- 1 gelatine sheet = 15ml measure of powder gelatine.

Decorative Tips

- Decorate with a chocolate collar.
- Spoon berries on the top.
- Crumb coat the outside with biscuit mixture or grated chocolate.
- Chocolate curls around the outside are lovely if you have the time to make them.

Note

If you are vegetarian the gelatine may be left out or agar agar can be used instead. Using gelatine gives the cake more stability in a hot and humid climate but it is the cream cheese and chocolate combination that actually sets the cake.

Chocolate Filling

Ingredients

2 tsp gelatine

2 cups couveture chocolate broken into small pieces

1 tsp pure vanilla extract

¼ cup brandy or Cointreau

¼ cup hot water

Method

1. Melt the chocolate on low in microwave being careful not to burn and stirring all the time between 20 second bursts of full microwave power.
2. Sprinkle the gelatine into ¼ cup of brandy – mix and stir well. Microwave on high for 30 seconds then stir again and add the ¼ cup boiling water.
3. Add gelatine mixture to the chocolate mixture and beat with an electric beater until well blended and thickened.

Notes

- This is perfect to sandwich between cake layers or to pour over ice cream desserts.
- Try substituting the alcohol with other flavours.
- The chocolate filling gives a lovely shine when used as a glaze.
- For vegetarians gelatine can be substituted with agar agar.

Dark Chocolate Ganache Cake

Ingredients

125g butter

210g castor sugar

3 large eggs

240g plain flour

120ml strong coffee

50g cocoa

5ml cream of tartar

5ml bi-carbonate of soda

1ml salt

250ml double cream yoghurt

Method

1. Pre-heat oven to 180°C.
2. Line the base and side of a 23cm diameter tin.
3. Cream the butter and castor sugar in an electric mixer until light and fluffy.
4. Add the egg yolks one by one, beating well after each addition.
5. To prevent the mix from curdling, add a tablespoon of flour after each egg yolk.
6. In a small bowl add the coffee to the cocoa powder and whisk until dissolved.
7. Add this to the butter mixture and continue beating until mixed.
8. Sift the flour, cream of tartar, bi-carb and salt together twice.
9. Lightly fold the dry ingredients, alternately with the yoghurt, into the mixture.
10. DO NOT OVERMIX.
11. Beat the egg whites in a separate bowl until they are at soft peak stage.
12. Fold the egg whites into the mixture using a metal spoon.
13. Spoon the mixture into the tin and bake for approximately 30 minutes at 180°C.
14. Allow the cake to cool before removing from the tin.

To Assemble

1. Cut the cake into 3 sections horizontally. Take care in doing this as the layers are very thin and easily broken.
2. Remove each layer carefully with the aid of a thin board equal to the size of the cake layer.
3. Fill each layer with the ganache. Let each layer harden individually and then stack the sections on top of one another ensuring that the flattest layer is on the top of the cake.
4. Finish the cake with a ganache topping or butter cream and cover with sugarpaste depending on the design you have chosen.

Ganache

Ingredients

500ml sour cream

50g butter

600g good moulding or couveture chocolate

Method

1. Combine the cream and chocolate into a bowl.
2. Heat the cream mixture to boiling point in a microwave oven.
3. Make sure you use the microwave on low and use short bursts of power.
4. Stir at intervals to make sure the chocolate and cream are well blended.
5. Stand to cool.
6. Place in the refrigerator and allow to set.

Tip for the Ganache

Should the weather be humid and very hot, use ⅔ chocolate to ⅓ cream to provide added stability underneath the sugarpaste.

Spicy Oil Cake

Ingredients

3 extra large eggs, separated

210g castor sugar

125ml sunflower oil

125ml unsweetened orange juice

5ml vanilla essence

3ml lemon essence

5ml ground cinnamon (optional)

5ml ground mixed spice (optional)

210g self raising flour, sifted

Method

1. Place egg yolks, castor sugar, oil and 2 essences in a mixing jug and beat well.
2. Add orange juice and beat further.
3. Whip egg whites until stiff.
4. Sift together the flour and the spices.
5. Pour yolk mixture into the flour mixture and fold in well.
6. Add stiffly beaten egg whites to batter mixture and fold in well.
7. Pour into a 20cm cake tin and bake for 1 hour at 100°C until firm to touch depending on oven.

Tips

- The essences can be substituted for other flavouring or essence and the spices left out for a simple sponge that keeps and cuts well.
- Alternatively the orange juice in this recipe can be substituted with a liqueur of your choice or simply water.
- Fan force convection ovens have a higher temperature than standard ovens. When using a fan force oven lower temperature by 20°C but use same baking time.
- Temperatures and baking times differ according to altitudes.

Fruit Cake

Ingredients

250g butter

250g soft brown sugar

6 large eggs

380g flour

Pinch of salt

2ml bi-carb soda

2½ml nutmeg

5ml cinnamon

Pinch of ground cloves

2½mls all spice

5ml ground ginger

100ml smooth apricot jam

250g bleached sultanas (yellow sultanas)

250g currants

250g seedless raisins

250g dates

100g pecan nuts

250g chopped glacé cherries

125g chopped mixed peel

150g glacé fruit – pineapple, ginger, watermelon, fig & apricot

125ml brandy

Method

1. Wash the dried fruit (raisins, sultanas, currants) gently in warm water to clean. Allow to dry.
2. Chop up dates, mixed peel, cherries and glacé fruit.
3. Mix all the fruits together (but not the nuts) and pour over the brandy. Cover the bowl with cling wrap, or put the fruit into a sealed container, and leave to macerate in the brandy overnight.
4. Sift the flour, spices, salt and bi-carb soda.
5. Cream the butter and sugar. Soft room temperature butter is best.
6. Add the eggs 1 at a time. After each egg add a tablespoon of flour to prevent the mix curdling.
7. Add the apricot jam. Stir in to blend and add the dry ingredients.
8. Add the nuts and then the mixed fruit. Blend well so that the fruit is evenly distributed.

Preparation

1. Line a 20cm tin with greaseproof paper.
2. Ensure that the paper fits well into the corners or curve of the tin you are using.
3. The outside of the tin may be lined with brown paper to ensure the cake bakes at a moderate, even temperature without burning.
4. Fill the prepared tin with cake mix ensuring the top is level.
5. Bake at 120°C for 3 to 4 hours.
6. When the cake has cooled remove from the tin and remove the paper.
7. Pour over 100ml of a brandy and van der hum mix (vd hum is an orange liqueur made in South Africa).
8. Allow the cake to mature for at least 4 weeks.

Tip

In place of alcohol you can use 100ml of orange juice and 15ml of glycerine (use a pure safe glycerine from the chemist). This will ensure the cake stays moist.

Boiled Fruit Cake

Ingredients

8 cups fruit cake mix or 3 cups currants, 3 cups raisins & 2 cups sultanas

2 cups dates

2 cups dark brown sugar

400g butter

5 eggs

¾ cup brandy

125g mixed peel

4 cups flour

2 tsp bi-carb soda

2 tsp mixed spices

2 tsp cinnamon

1 tsp nutmeg

2 tsp baking powder

1 tsp ginger

Pinch of ground cloves

300g cherries

300g nuts – walnut, pecan or almond (Optional – can be omitted for nut allergies)

Method

1. Boil fruit, butter, sugar and 2 cups of water for 20 minutes.
2. Cool and add 2 tsp bi-carb soda.
3. Add chopped cherries, nuts and mixed peel.
4. Beat eggs and add to fruit mixture.
5. Add all dry ingredients and combine to make a wet mixture.
6. Add the brandy and stir thoroughly.
7. Line a baking tin well using greaseproof paper cut to fit the pan.
8. Pour the cake mixture into the pan.
9. Put 2 tbs of water or brandy on top of raw cake mix and even the mix with the back of a large spoon before putting in oven. This helps to prevent burning.
10. Bang the tin well on a flat surface to even out the cake mixture before putting it in the oven.

11. A piece of wet cardboard can be placed underneath the tin. This helps retain moisture.
12. Bake at 150°C for about 2 hours depending on the size of the cake and oven. See note.
13. After the first hour a piece of cardboard can be placed on the top of the tin. This prevents the top of the cake from drying out and keeps the cake from rising too much.
14. When the cake is firm to the touch it is time to take it out of the oven.
15. Test with a skewer before removing from oven.
16. Remove from the oven and turn upside down immediately. This ensures that the top (that may sometimes rise) is flattened while the cake is still warm and retains its shape.
17. When cool wrap in baking paper and pour another cup or 2 of brandy and orange liqueur mixed together over the cake. Seal and wrap in foil. Leave to mature for 2-3 months in a cool place (not the fridge).

Tip

Make sure that you lower the temperature of the oven by 20°C if the oven is fan forced as a fan forced oven cooks a lot quicker.

Note

This cake is suitable for 1 x 25cm square or 2 x 20cm round tins (25cm=10", 20cm=8").

Carrot Cake

Ingredients

5 eggs

1¾ cups castor sugar

1½ cups sunflower oil

2 cups plain flour

1 cup self raising flour

2 level tsp bi-carb soda

3 level tsp of cinnamon

Pinch of salt

1 cup chopped pecans

1 cup mixed fruit – sultanas, raisins, currants

3 cups grated carrot

Method

1. Grease a baking tin 25cm by 28cm and 7cm deep.
2. Line with grease-proof paper making sure the corners are neat and sharp.
3. Break eggs into a large bowl.
4. Add sugar and stir with a wooden spoon to dissolve.
5. Add oil.
6. Add sifted flour, bi-carb soda, cinnamon and salt.
7. Stir to blend the ingredients well.
8. Add nuts, fruit and grated carrot.
9. Stir to mix the ingredients well but do not beat with an electric beater.
10. Pour into the prepared tin.
11. Spread evenly so the mix is level.
12. Bake in a moderate 170°C oven for approximately 1½ hours.
13. Allow to cool in the tin until it is quite cold.

Cream Cheese Icing

Ingredients

2 x 250ml tubs of full cream smooth cream cheese

250g pure butter

3-4 cups (750ml) icing sugar

Method

1. Melt butter and add to the cream cheese.
2. Mix together using a beater.
3. Add icing sugar 1 cup at a time until the icing is creamy and holds its shape well.
4. Use as a filling and to top the cake.

Note

Fat free cream cheese can be used however the end result may be a lot softer.

Butter Cream Icing – Option 1

Ingredients

450g sifted icing sugar

100g butter

10ml corn starch

5ml vanilla essence or any flavouring or essence

Add enough liquid such as coffee, orange juice or liqueur to complement the taste and achieve a spreading consistency.

Method

1. Cream the butter well with an electric beater.
2. Mix the corn starch with a little of the chosen liquid and the essence.
3. Add to the creamed butter and beat well.
4. Add the remaining icing sugar and beat, adding extra liquid if necessary to achieve a spreading consistency.
5. The repetitive beating will result in a light fluffy consistency and the corn starch will stabilise the oils in a hot climate. This may be omitted if in a cooler climate.

Butter Cream Icing – Option 2

Ingredients

2 egg whites

25g castor sugar

100g granulated sugar

50ml water

200g unsalted butter (soft)

Method

1. Beat the egg whites until stiff peak.
2. Add the castor sugar in a thin stream while beating the egg white.
3. Boil the sugar and water together. The temperature should reach 116°C.
4. Test a little piece in cold water – the sugar stage you want is soft ball.
5. When the sugar is at the correct stage, pour the slightly cooled sugar syrup into the meringue mix while whisking.
6. Continue to whisk until the mixture is cool.
7. The mixture should be firm and thick.
8. Beat the butter until soft and smooth.
9. Then beat the butter into the egg mix to make a soft butter cream.

Tip

Flavourings such as vanilla, almond, rum or nuts can be added to this cream.

Frosted Icing

(7 minute frosting or foam frosting)

This light icing is like soft meringue. The top sets with a soft crust. It can be swirled on top of cupcakes and also be used on children's party cakes and special occasion cakes.

Ingredients

375ml white castor sugar

2 egg whites

80ml cold water

1ml cream of tartar

Pinch salt

2ml vanilla essence

Method

1. Combine all the ingredients except the vanilla in the top of a double boiler.
2. Beat to mix well.
3. Place over boiling water.
4. Beat continuously until mixture forms a frosted soft peak. Make sure that the side and the bottom is stirred approximately 3 times so that the icing does not cook quicker in these places.
5. Remove from the heat, add vanilla and use immediately.

Note

Do not cook any longer than necessary. The mixture will crystallise easily so watch it at all times.

Marzipan Recipe

Ingredients

2 cups granulated sugar

2ml cream of tartar

4 cups finely ground almonds

2 egg whites

3ml almond essence

12.5ml food grade glycerine

Method

1. Place the sugar and water in a clean pot. If possible use a pot that is kept just for sugar work. (If the pot is dirty the sugar syrup will crystallise.)
2. Add the cream of tartar.
3. Bring the sugar and water to a rapid boil.
4. Continue to soft ball stage (sugar should make a soft ball if dropped into cold water).
5. Once the sugar is ready add to the ground almonds and egg white.
6. Mix well and add the glycerine and essence.
7. Knead into a soft pliable ball.
8. Wrap in plastic wrap until needed to keep the almond paste soft and pliable.

Coffee Gateaux Filling

Ingredients

125g sugar

25ml water

4 egg yolks

240g unsalted butter

15ml (3 tsp) instant coffee dissolved in 10ml (2 tsp) hot water

Method

1. Dissolve sugar in water in a pan over heat until it starts to thicken.
2. Swirl around in the pan until it is quite thick and slightly golden.
3. Beat egg yolks and add sugar syrup.
4. Beat until thick and creamy.
5. Cream butter and add egg and sugar mixture to it.
6. Add coffee. This recipe thickens on cooling.

Tip

As an alternative, mix chocolate and marzipan to a paste consistency then add the above mixture and spread over the gateaux layers. Let it cool and harden then cover with fondant.

Edible Glitter

1. Dissolve 2 tsp of Gum Arabic in ⅓ cup of water and add the colour you want.
2. Paint on a sheet of glass and allow to dry.
3. Scrape off and crush to form edible glitter.

Glaze For Cakes

1. Dissolve 30ml of Tylose powder in 125ml of cold water over hot water.
2. Stir frequently and allow to cool.
3. Melt 12.5ml of sugar in 5ml of water. Bring to the boil.
4. Cool and add 30ml of pure alcohol.
5. Add the 2 mixes together.
6. Strain and keep in a bottle.

Flower Paste

Ingredients

1 egg white

Pure icing sugar (approximately 300g)

Solidified vegetable oil or petal base

Tylose powder (Tylopur) superior grade

1 tsp copha

Method

1. Mix egg white and sufficient icing sugar to form a stiff peak royal icing.
2. Add 2 well rounded tsp of Tylose powder and mix through well.
3. Wash hands thoroughly. Put 1 rounded tsp of copha into your hands and work paste thoroughly for at least 5 minutes.
4. It may be a good idea to mix 2 individual golf size balls separately to facilitate easier blending.
5. Wrap in cling wrap and store in an airtight container. Paste does not need to be kept in the fridge.

Note

This paste will be unusable if it is not worked well in the making process as it will have no stretch. If you do you work it well, you will be able to roll it out paper thin.

Cooked Flower Paste

Ingredients

500ml sifted icing sugar

1 level dsp (12ml) gelatine

1 tsp (5ml) Tylose powder or Gum Tragacanth

1 medium egg white (45ml) slightly beaten

2 tblsp (30ml) cold water

Method

1. Rub the mixer bowl with white vegetable fat.
2. Sieve 1 cup of icing sugar into the greased bowl. Add the Tylose powder to the icing sugar.
3. Microwave the mixture for 2-3 minutes on medium setting stirring in between the warming period. Heat to body temperature. Place a clean finger into the powder. If it feels a little hot then it is above body temperature.
4. Sprinkle the gelatine over the water in a small bowl and allow to sponge. Place the sponged gelatine over hot water until it is clear.
5. When the icing is the right temperature, add the slightly beaten egg white and the gelatine mixture and beat until all the ingredients are combined using an electric beater.
6. At this stage all the ingredients will be a grey/beige colour. Turn the beater to maximum speed and beat until the mixture becomes stringy.
7. Gradually add the remaining icing sugar.
8. When all the icing sugar has been well mixed, the mixture will turn white. At this stage put a little vegetable fat on clean hands and work the mixture for approximately 10 minutes. This will make the paste very elastic.
9. Rub a little vegetable fat on the outside of the paste. Place in a plastic bag and then in an airtight container and store in the fridge. The paste will be ready for use after 24 hours.
10. When using the paste only cut off a small piece and then work it well prior to rolling it out. Always keep paste in a sealed plastic bag when not in use.

Mexican Paste

Mexican paste is used for architectural work and making of plaques, ribbons, clothes and many more similar applications. It dries hard quickly and is very brittle, therefore it is not suitable for use in flower making.

Ingredients

250g icing sugar mix

15ml Tylose powder (Tylopur) superior grade

5ml liquid glucose

30ml cold water

Vegetable fat/petal base (enough for paste not to stick to hands).

Method

1. Mix the Tylose powder and icing sugar together and add liquid glucose and water.
2. Put petal base on hands and work into the icing sugar mixture. Knead well.
3. Place in a sealed plastic bag within a non-porous container in the fridge.
4. Leave for 24 hours to get best results.

Tip

Measure your icing sugar on a scale as a cup measurement does not weigh 250g. The paste will be very soft and sticky if accurate measurements are not adhered to.

Flower Paste w. Liquid Glucose

Ingredients

62ml (short ¼ cup) cold water

2 level tsp (10ml) gelatine

2 rounded tsp (12ml) of liquid glucose – slightly warmed

2 cups (500ml) sifted icing sugar (plus a little more if necessary)

1 tsp (5ml) Tylose powder (Tylopur) superior grade

1 tsp (5ml) vegetable fat or Petal Base

Method

1. Sponge the gelatine in the water and then place over hot water to dissolve completely.
2. Add the warmed liquid glucose to the clear gelatine mixture.
3. Pour the liquid into the icing sugar.
4. Work well by kneading. At this stage it feels like putty.
5. Add more sifted icing sugar if a little sticky.
6. Add one tsp of Tylopur and one tsp of vegetable fat and continue to work thoroughly. The paste will stiffen up while working and become a little rubbery on stretching.
7. When ready to use, slice a small piece off and work it up by dipping it in a little water.

Trouble Shooting

Cake Covering Problems

Problem: Grazes appear when covering a cake with sugarpaste.

Solution: Rub the area gently and quickly in one direction with a finger. A little vegetable fat may re-moisten the area temporarily but do not use too much as it could become rancid if the cake is left for some time before being eaten. Secondly, sprinkle the area with a little icing sugar – this will absorb the moisture and seal the area.

Problem: Hairline cracks on freshly rolled sugarpaste.

Solution: To eliminate hairline cracks use a little cooking oil on your hands before polishing your cake and the cracks will disappear.

Problem: Sweating of sugarpaste.

Solution: Ensure the cake is at room temperature before covering. Leave the cake to reabsorb moisture (do not wipe) from sugarpaste and stand near a breeze or cool fan to hasten the process.

Royal Icing Problems

Problem: Piped work does not keep its shape and becomes glassy looking.

Reason: Royal icing consistency is too soft.

Solution: Slowly add more icing sugar while beating to achieve the correct consistency.

Problem: Royal icing dries very quickly when piping.

Reason: Royal icing has been made incorrectly – icing sugar has been added too quickly and/or quantities added at one time are too great.

Solution: Beat thoroughly between each addition to achieve best results and a light consistency that will not be heavy on the hands when piping.

Material piping bags are porous and let air in which dries the icing too quickly. Material bags also harbour bacteria, therefore it is better to use silicone paper bags.

Paste Problems

Problem: Flower paste is dry and crumbly.

Reason:
- Not worked enough in the making.
- Royal icing too stiff to begin with.
- Too much fat has been used.
- Too much Tylose powder has been used.

Solution: For all of the above, add egg white to work up to required consistency. A little water can also be used but egg white is best as it retains its strength.

Alternatively, with hard paste, add a small quantity of commercial sugarpaste and work in well.

Problem: Cracks in paste.

Solution: To remove deep set cracks in balls of paste, work paste very well between the fingers and then roll firmly in the palm of the hand in a circular motion.

Problem: Soft flower paste.

Reason: Too little Tylose powder has been added or the royal icing consistency is too soft.

Solution: Add more icing sugar or a little Tylose powder and work it in well.

Problem: Mexican Paste is too sticky.

Reason: Incorrect measurement of ingredients.

Solution: 15ml is not 15g – use what the recipe says in measurement.

Dirty Marks

Problem: Dirty marks appear on your work.

Reason: This may be in the form of powder colour or dirt of some kind.

Solution: Apply a little isopropyl alcohol/ rose spirit or surgical spirits on a cotton wool ball and gently rub the mark away.

Stained Hands

Problem: Hands are stained after colouring dark paste.

Solution: Dampen the hands with a little water. Sprinkle a little washing soda onto the hands. They will feel warm instantly. Rub the affected area and then run under water. The stain will disappear.

Helpful Hints

Prevent Paste Drying Out

- Rub a little fat on the outside of flower paste prior to storage as this prevents the paste drying while being stored.
- Keep in a plastic bag inside a plastic container.
- Keep a tiny glass container upturned on your board and put pieces of paste underneath as you are working so they will not dry out.

Sugarpaste Finishing Touches

- X-ray plates or semi flexible plastic matting gives a silky smooth finish to the cakes.
- Rub a little vegetable oil between the hands and then onto the surface of the sugarpaste. This gives a lovely non-matt look to the cake without being too glossy.

Lighting & Airflow

- Work under a daylight bulb – it is light blue and seems to help.
- Never cover a cake in night-light as the imperfections will not be visible. Cakes must always be covered in daylight.
- Cover cakes in a still environment – fans, breezes or air conditioning will cause the covering to dry out too quickly.

Piping Lace Points

- Pipe the lace pieces directly on acetate paper or cellophane – it is see-through and they release easily.

Royal Icing

- Store in a jar. Place a piece of damp cloth over the top before screwing down the lid – it will keep for a day or two.

Snail Trail

- If you are using a colour, thin down sugarpaste to piping consistency with a little water. This way the snail trail will be exactly the same colour as the cake.

Succulents

- To make succulent flowers bake the sugarpaste in the oven at a temperature of 100°C for approximately 10 minutes until it bubbles.

Sticky Paste And Humidity

Flower paste is temperamental in changing weather conditions. This is normal and therefore some quick-fix solutions can be applied.

- Apply a little cornflour on your hands and work into the paste. This will absorb some of the moisture and prevent sticking. Never add too much fat as this will make the problem worse and dry out the paste.
- In very humid weather a little more Tylose powder needs to be added to the paste. This is a sugar-shortening agent and therefore more water will be absorbed by the paste before it flops.
- To dry flower paste quickly and keep it stable, place the wet paste item on a piece of sponge and place it in the oven for 5 minutes at 50°C. Let it cool and place it immediately in a cardboard or polystyrene box until required. Plastic can cause flowers to sweat and black spots can appear on the paste.
- Using too much fat will also weaken the paste and cause it to flop quicker.
- If there is an excessive amount of damp in the area where your flowers are stored, keep silicone sachets and bi-carbonate of soda in the same box as the flowers.
- Leave sugarpaste items in a wardrobe or cupboard which has a light in it. Close the door and leave overnight. This will dry out any moisture in the environment.
- A dehumidifier also works well.

Clean Edges

- To prevent furry edges when using blunt cutters, scrape the cut out paste object and cutter down the edge of the board. This gives an exceptionally clean cut.
- Lay thinly rolled paste on top of a cutter and roll over the cutter. Use your thumb to rub over the edge before you remove the shape.
- Cut out the paste item and then lift the paste and cutter up together. Rub a little fat against the cutter edges and release the shape.

Taping

- When taping flowers together, wind the ¼ width tape around the wire a couple of millimetres below the flower or leaf a few times then slip the sleeve of tape right up to where the flower joins the wire. You will get a very neat join.
- When taping is completed, over-tape the wires with a full width tape. This will ensure a neat and professional finish.

Ribbon

- To fix paste ribbon to a cake, dampen the ribbon not the cake.

Sprays

- A spray of wired flowers can be inserted into a cake by placing them in a length of plastic straw.
- A cell pick or posy pick can also be used but never insert bare wires into a cake.

Clean Brushes

- When dusting flowers with different colours, clean off brushes by using cornflour instead of washing them.

Sealing Colours

- Wipe Vaseline around the top of paste colour jars to stop the colours seeping.

Berries

- When making balls or berries cut your paste with a flower cutter then roll the paste into a ball. This will ensure they are all the same size.

Whiskers

- To make whiskers on a small mouse or rabbit, thread a needle with a double strand of cotton and the gently thread through the snout.

Adding Colour to Royal Icing

- Add colour to royal icing when it is at peaking consistency.
- Colour 2 shades lighter than the one you need, as the colours continue to darken in the mixture for 10 minutes or so before the final shade is attained.

Mixing Shades

- Take 1 ball of the desired colour in the deepest shade.
- Have 3 balls of white paste all the same size.
- Halve the deepest colour and add to the first ball of white paste to obtain shade 1.
- Halve the ball that has just been coloured and add to the next ball of white to obtain shade 2.
- Halve this ball of paste and add to the last ball of white.
- In this way you get even shading.

Piped Dots

- Add a drop or 2 of glycerine to 1 tbs medium peak royal icing to prevent peaks on dots.
- Pipe the dot at an angle just off 90°.
- Pipe the ball with even pressure and then release pressure on the bag and take the tip of the tube away from the icing.

Colour Setting

- Dusted powder colours can bleed when glaze is sprayed on them to give a shiny finish. Set the colours by steaming them over a boiling kettle or pot very quickly and then spray with glaze mixture.
- When adding powder colours to paste make up a small ball a few shades darker than the colour you want. Allow the ball of coloured paste to rest for 30 minutes, then knead well and add the small ball of coloured paste to white flower paste in the quantity you require. This will ensure that your paste will not have colour streaks or spots and you will reach the perfect shade you require.
- Mix enough coloured paste to complete the whole project as it is difficult to match colours later on.
- When colouring paste, cut a piece in half to check that the colour is mixed.

Colour and Classification

How to use powder colours in fondant and on flower paste

- To colour paste, dip paste in liquid, put a little petal base or vegetable fat on your finger and then dip the paste in powder colour. Work the powder colour into a small area and then work it through the entire paste.
- If paste becomes dry when colour is added to it, soften by mixing in a little egg white. Water also works well but egg white strengthens the paste. Be careful not to use too much egg white as it will cause the paste to become rubber-like.
- Blend colours with cornflour or rice flour to break down the concentration of colour.
- Mix correct colour match on a double white tissue and then do a swatch test on a piece of paste before applying to the finished product.
- Black powder must always be mixed with a small amount of liquid to achieve true black and the liquid then added to the paste.

Sir Isaac Newton invented the colour wheel, which is made up of primary, secondary and tertiary colours. He associated each colour in the wheel with different musical notes and the individual colours are said to portray separate psychological effects in human emotion.

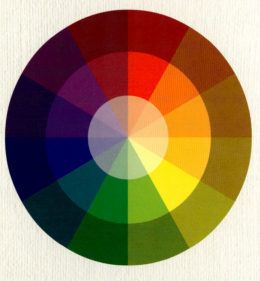

1. P blue (powder blue)
2. Magic blue sparkle
3. Turquoise
4. Blue
5. Rubine
6. Magic pale pink sparkle
7. P pink (pale pink)
8. Rose
9. Lemon
10. Yellow
11. Magic lemon sparkle
12. Gold (lustre)
13. Flesh
14. Copper (lustre)
15. Brown
16. Silver (lustre)
17. Black